Letters to My Hypothetical Children:

Life Lessons, Making Mistakes, & Keeping it Real

Marcia Allyn Luke

Letters to My Hypothetical Children

Twin Horseshoes Publishing
www.twinhorseshoes.ca
Ontario, Canada

Copyright © Letters to My Hypothetical Children: Life Lessons, Making Mistakes, and Keeping it Real, 2021

All rights reserved. Without limiting the rights under copyright reserved above, no part of this publication may be reproduced, stored in, or introduced into a retrieval system, or transmitted in any form or by any means (electronic, mechanical, including photocopying, recording or otherwise), without the prior written permission of both the copyright owner and the above publisher of this book.

This publication contains the opinions and ideas of its author and is designed to provide useful information in regard to the subject matter covered. The author and publisher are not engaged in health or other professional services in this publication. This publication is not intended to provide a basis for action in particular circumstances without consideration by a competent professional. The author and publisher expressly disclaim any responsibility for any liability, loss, or risk, personal or otherwise, which is incurred as a consequence, directly or indirectly, of the use and application of any of the contents of this book. While the author has made every effort to provide accurate information at publication time, the publisher and the author assume no responsibility for author or third-party websites or their content.

Luke, Marcia Allyn
Letters to My Hypothetical Children: Life Lessons, Making Mistakes, and Keeping it Real
Includes bibliographical references.

eBook ISBN 978-1-7775345-16
Paperback ISBN 978-1-7775345-09

Nonfiction | Biography & Autobiography | Personal Memoirs
Nonfiction | Family & Relationships | General
Nonfiction | Humour | Topic | Marriage & Family

This book is sold subject to the condition that it shall not, by way of trade or otherwise, be lent, re-sold, hired out, or otherwise circulated without the publisher's prior consent in any form of binding or cover other than that in which it is published and without a similar condition including this condition being imposed on the subsequent purchase.

Letters to My Hypothetical Children

Table of Contents

Foreword .... - 7 -
Daisy-Mae Hamelinck .... - 7 -
Preface .... - 10 -
Chapter 1 .... - 15 -
   You can take the girl out of the country .... - 15 -
   A tired dog is a happy dog (and kids too) .... - 21 -
   Honesty is the best policy .... - 28 -
   Don't lie to your parents .... - 30 -
   Do you know where your children are? .... - 33 -
   Don't drink on an empty stomach .... - 37 -
   Know your limit, stay within it .... - 41 -
Chapter 2 .... - 44 -
   Not too cool for school .... - 44 -
   Don't judge a book by its cover .... - 46 -
   If at first you don't succeed, try, try again .... - 51 -
   Never stop learning .... - 58 -
Chapter 3 .... - 61 -
   If you love what you do, you'll never work a day in your life - 61 -
   Doors open when you know someone; don't close them .... - 65 -
   Help your kids out, but make sure they bust their butt .... - 69 -
   Ask the tough questions .... - 76 -
   Don't give up .... - 80 -

Look at the kid that's in front of you .... - 82 -

Chapter 4 .... - 88 -

A penny saved is a penny earned .... - 88 -

To get a little, you have to give a little .... - 90 -

It pays to take good care of your belongings .... - 93 -

Do things with your kids, not for them .... - 101 -

Sometimes keeping busy is a distraction .... - 103 -

Experiences have more value than money .... - 105 -

Sometimes your expectations need a reality check .... - 107 -

Chapter 5 .... - 109 -

Grant me the serenity to accept the things I cannot change ... - 109 -

Find a place that brings you peace .... - 114 -

Music connects with your soul .... - 120 -

Death is just the next chapter .... - 124 -

Pets are family members too .... - 126 -

Chapter 6 .... - 132 -

Take care of your body; it's the only one you get .... - 132 -

Watch where you're going .... - 134 -

If I only had a brain…or a new one .... - 138 -

If you're not sure, just go to the hospital .... - 140 -

Children are parasites .... - 147 -

Ask for help .... - 150 -

Listen to your body .... - 152 -

- Read a book .... - 160 -
- If you hear it once, it's a coincidence .... - 162 -

Chapter 7 .... - 165 -
- It takes one to know one .... - 165 -
- Time spent is more important than what you do .... - 167 -
- R.E.S.P.E.C.T. .... - 173 -
- Avoid office politics and place your trust carefully .... - 179 -
- Sometimes good things come from hitting rock bottom .... - 182 -
- Shared experiences create deep connections .... - 185 -
- Fandom creates a unique shared language .... - 189 -
- Love is all you need .... - 192 -
- It really is: "treat others the way you want to be treated" ...... - 195 -

Chapter 8 .... - 198 -
- What doesn't kill you makes you stronger .... - 198 -
- Love hurts .... - 200 -
- The birds and the bees .... - 205 -
- Make sure you don't wait to have the sex talk .... - 209 -
- If you want real change, you have to tear down the castle .... - 217 -

Epilogue .... - 222 -
- Dear Cami and Maya .... - 222 -

Acknowledgements .... - 225 -
- Twin Horseshoes .... - 225 -

About the Author .... - 227 -
- Marcia Allyn Luke .... - 227 -

Notes.. - 230 -

Foreword

Daisy-Mae Hamelinck
OCT, M.A., B.Ed., B.A. (Hons), SSWD

Marcia Allyn Luke's *Letters to My Hypothetical Children: Life Lessons, Making Mistakes, and Keeping it Real* is a book about growth and one strong woman's personal journey in forging her path—personally and professionally. Marcia's story is about finding one's passion and the discoveries (and misadventures) along the way.

Letters to My Hypothetical Children: Life Lessons, Making Mistakes, and Keeping it Real has the Canadian country, and more specifically, the landscapes of Ontario, as the backdrop to this biographical true story. This is a story full of many themes regarding coming of age, innocence (and loss thereof), facing uncertainty, and honouring one's truth. Marcia reminds us how important it is to be open on the journey—and how one can find the leader within when one examines what *authentically* moves the heart, soul, and spirit.

Through childhood memories, Marcia teaches us how to pause and look back at one's past in order to better understand, and appreciate, the present. Marcia puts a microscope on her childhood and upbringing, and the various moments she 'felt were right', along with the places, and people, that did not.

Marcia shares her successes and reminds us to stand at 'the doors' that may have been closed by parents, genetics, or within oneself, through fear and self-doubt. She encourages us to look beyond those 'closed doors' and make life more about rebuilding or 'tearing down the castle'.

In many ways, this story is the journey of a leader-in-the-making, changing what was once a whisper in her soul, to a voice of advocacy and awareness-raising in her community via the means she knows well—through storytelling.

Marcia's writing is raw, real, and her humour shines through, especially when it comes to tough stuff like managing concussions, postpartum depression, relationship breakdown, medical visits, and of course, her journey with infertility. Thus, birthing the idea to 'write to her hypothetical children'.

Marcia's past, mistakes, and lessons learned in life, help her cope with the various struggles and stressors that come her way as she writes to her twins, Cami and Maya. Not only does she want to pass these 'gems' onto her children, but she also wants to share them with anyone and everyone.

What really makes this book stand out above the rest, is that it literally includes *three stories in one*. The book has been formatted in a particular way so that it can be read as a series of life lessons, parenting perspectives, or the true story of a Canadian country girl. Each of these angles are intertwined and even the photos in each chapter tell a special story. You can literally choose to read only the life lessons OR the parenting perspectives OR the biographical story, OR, for some, perhaps only the pictures!

Letters to My Hypothetical Children: Life Lessons, Making Mistakes, and Keeping it Real will remind readers of their own amazing journey through life. This book is a true Canadian gem and a priceless gift to her once 'hypothetical children'.

Marcia's story is truly everyone's story—a story of life lessons, making mistakes, and keeping it real.

Preface

I was trying to get pregnant, and having difficulty staying pregnant, when I came up with the idea for this book. When I started writing, I didn't know if I would ever become a parent, which is why this book is to my 'hypothetical' children. I was deep in thought about what kind of parent I would become, and I felt the need to share the life lessons I've learned with my hypothetical children. That's what a parent does, right? Guide their children based on their own experiences? The problem is, then I would have to admit to my mistakes and divulge information that I felt shouldn't necessarily come from a parent (at least not the ideal parent I imagined then). This is the important stuff, and it should be shared, but I've always been better at writing, so this book is my way to communicate all these gems: lessons learned, mistakes I've made, and told in an honest, call-it-like-it-is manner.

There's something intimate about a letter: the familiar handwriting, the smell of the person who wrote it, the feel of the paper in your hands, even the excitement of receiving mail. I have several reasons why I call these pages 'letters. The first is that when I was a teenager, I would write letters to my friends, or boyfriends, and before texting, this was the way we communicated what we thought was important information. I also wrote letters to my grandma when I was away at university, so it became nostalgic for that reason. Finally, I didn't really write in a journal or diary, but I would write letters when I was upset and needed to process my emotions. Often the letter would be thrown out or burned, but it became a way of processing and articulating strong emotions. That's why I call this book a series of letters.

This book is organized in two different ways. The first is that the chapters roughly align with the eight dimensions of wellness [1] : environmental (Chapter 1), intellectual (Chapter 2), occupational (Chapter 3), financial (Chapter 4), spiritual (Chapter 5), physical (Chapter 6), social (Chapter 7), and emotional (Chapter 8). I tried to group the stories into themes, and these were the themes that made the most sense to me. That's why there are eight chapters. Because it's organized in themes, there will be some repetition of stories from different perspectives (I'll try to keep it to a minimum!). The second structure is within each chapter: life lessons, parenting perspectives,

---

[1] Swarbick, M. (2006). A Wellness Approach. *Psychiatric Rehabilitation Journal, 29*(4), 311-314.

and stories. The life lessons are for my daughters (Maya and Cami) when they are old enough and teenagers everywhere, the parenting perspectives are for parents and reminders for myself, and the stories are examples of these in between and all around. So really, you can read some, or all, of these in any order that you want; it's like three books in one!

Maya and Cami, this book is for you. Take these stories and do with them what you will. Some of these are things I wished my parents had told me, some of these would be regrets (if I believed in regrets), and some of these stories will hopefully correct misinformation. These are my experiences, so take them with a grain of salt. You are different from me, so you may never need the information in these pages. In fact, I hope you don't. But some pages you will need and if there is ever any doubt in your mind that I was once young or flawed, you will soon know otherwise. And I hope you will know from this book that you can talk to me about anything, no matter how difficult. Or, if you can't, write me a letter and I'll write back.

Six Months' Pregnant

Even though I feared I would never have children, I did get pregnant with the help of modern medical science and fertility treatment. My journey getting pregnant and having twins is a big part of the reason for this book and its contents. Plus, look how $%^&-ing big my belly is!*

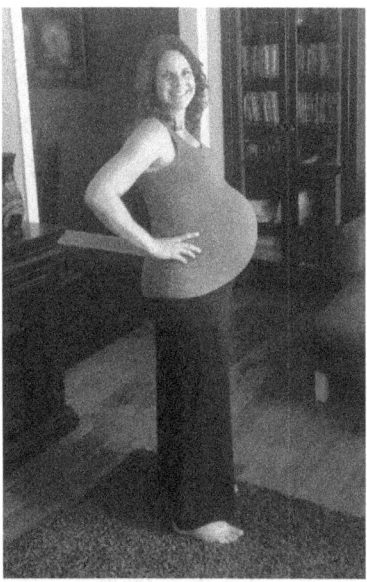

Photo Credit: Marcia Allyn Luke

To my parents, you did a wonderful job raising me and you gave me so much. This book is certainly not a negative comment on my childhood or your parenting skills. It's more about my fears as a parent and the standard that you set because you set the bar pretty high. In fact, you will find some amazing memories in these pages. You are also wonderful grandparents and I hope that if my girls can't talk to me about something, they will be able to talk to you.

For everyone else who picks up this book: I hope you feel a little less alone and a little more hopeful. I hope you maybe even laugh a little. I've often wondered if I'm screwing up my children. I've felt like a horrible parent. I have even felt like a horrible teenager! I hope that this book gives you the courage to talk to your kids about the hard stuff. I hope it starts a new conversation. Parenting today isn't what it was when my parents raised me. Kids have access to so much information and as parents we need to be a big part of the information pie. I even hope that some teenagers read this book so they can find the courage to talk to their parents. Every generation hopes that they can do things a little better than the generation before and I'm doing that the only way I know how, by writing.

Chapter 1

You can take the girl out of the country …but you can't take the country out of the girl

Your roots are important to understand and appreciate. They are a big part of who you are and who you become. You may decide that where you started out, isn't the life for you. You may decide on something totally different. It's not all or nothing, there are many degrees and variations in between. The most important thing is to listen to yourself. If you feel at peace in a place, go there. If the hustle and bustle of a busy city stresses you out, leave. Do what's best for you. I will never regret living in the city—I needed to experience it to know where I wanted to be. I've always loved farm fields and hay bales, in particular. They look so picturesque and tidy, wrapped up and spaced out in the fields. It doesn't matter if they are round or square, they make me smile and remind me of home.

Photo Credit: Skitterphoto from Pexels

I grew up in a small town in Southern Ontario. Actually, I grew up outside of the small town, surrounded by farm fields. And when I was eight years old, my parents decided it was getting too 'built up' and we moved. We moved further outside of an even smaller town halfway between civilization and the beginnings of cottage country. Our house was on a dirt road with a grand total of eight houses. It was also a dead-end road and it had no name. Our property line was next to a farm field and the cows would come right up to the fence. We had no need for curtains, since there was no one around to see anything. People found our house by "turning at the asparagus farm on the corner" and "if you get to the train tracks you've gone too far." I was nine when we moved in and excited at the prospect of a larger bedroom and a new house, but nervous about a new school and making friends.

Let's start with my family. My dad is about six feet tall, lean, and has always had a receding hairline. When I was young, his hair was light-ish brown, but now it's almost all white. I get my brown eyes from him, as well as my ability to tan. In the summer, sometimes he looks like a completely different ethnic background even though we're as white as it gets (English, Irish, Scottish mix). Growing up, my dad would go to work and then come home and work in his shop; he's an auto body worker. He still loves tinkering with cars, especially classic cars. He's extremely creative; he can look at a problem with a car, house, anything really, and figure out a way to 'MacGyver' it. It might not be exactly to code, but it's probably sturdier than regulation requires.

My dad called me 'pup' when I was young and then 'BUZZ BOM' when I got a bit older. Pup is self-explanatory, I think, but BUZZ BOM was a result of my pace of doing things. I heard "slow down" more than any phrase from my parents. My dad always said that I ran around like a chicken with my head cut off; I had only two speeds, on and off. My parents had BUZZ BOM made as a license plate for me (hence the capitalization). That being said, I'm fairly certain I inherited this particular trait from my dad. My mom's pace was always deliberate and planned, not necessarily slow, but steady.

I also have a sister, three and a half years older, who has always played an important role in my life. She's tall and lean, like my dad, with bright blue eyes and brown hair. She's had short hair for most of her life and it suits her well. She used to tell me that I was adopted because I didn't look like either of my parents. And it was true, so for quite some time she had me convinced that if I was bad, they would give me back. We got along great growing up, until our teenage years. I was 14 and she was 18; I was making plans for the weekend and she was focused on planning her future. The gap in maturity at that stage really drove a wedge between us. During that time, we fought, but when she went away to college, I realized how much I missed her and after that we were more than just sisters, we were friends. When I was young, I looked up to her, copied everything she did, and wanted nothing more than to spend all my time with her and her friends, which was likely incredibly annoying.

Last but certainly not least, my mom. My mom is a little taller than my five foot, five inches and we have a similar body type: a little more junk in the trunk, so to speak. She has soft hazel eyes and I get my curly hair from her. She and my sister have fairer skin, so they burn more easily. I get my academic nature from my mom as well. We both love books and school, we follow the rules and do well at most everything we attempt. My mom set the bar exceedingly high—her patience and diplomacy are out of this world. She loves hosting and takes great satisfaction from feeding people. She is also an excellent person with a high moral standard and a kindness that would rival Mother Theresa.

My parents provided my sister and I with many travelling opportunities when we were growing up. All of these were road trips, in a truck and trailer. It started out with a tent trailer, which was very much like camping. We would go to provincial parks and ride our bikes, explore nature, enjoy campfires, and play board games. Then the tent trailer became a travel trailer with bunk beds, which was cool. The travel trailer has enough room for my grandma to come along and since my grandpa didn't really enjoy travelling, she seized the opportunity often. Sometimes it was just for the weekend, but in the summer or for March break we would go on longer trips, and these were the ones my grandma loved.

We went to the East coast twice, once when I was five and once when I was 12. We climbed the stairs to the Plains of Abraham in Quebec, we saw the Hopewell Rocks in New Brunswick, we explored Green Gables in Prince Edward Island (PEI), we saw Peggy's Cove in Nova Scotia. The East coast is my favourite; it embodies a slower, friendlier pace of life. We went to the West coast when I was eight. We visited Butchart Gardens and stood next to the enormous Douglas Fir trees on Vancouver Island, British Columbia (BC); we took a dip in the hot springs and walked the Columbia Icefield glaciers in Banff National Park, Alberta; we saw the Bison beside the highway in Manitoba; we drove through the canola fields in Saskatchewan. What I loved about the West coast was the variations in scenery: plains to mountains, to forests, lakes, and the ocean. We went North to Kenora, Ontario when I was 15 and, on the way, rode the Algoma Railway which toured the Agawa Canyon. That was a particularly memorable trip since I was sick that day and ended up seeing more of the train's toilet than the scenery.

Parenting Perspective
A tired dog is a happy dog (and kids too)

Sometimes that means burning yourself out too. Use bait. For example, we would often go to Winterlude in Ottawa. They had delicious pastries called Beavertails, which are now in many places across Canada and offered in many variations. Originally, they were an Ottawa thing, and it was simply a piece of dough the shape of a beaver's tail, deep fried, and coated in sugar and cinnamon. Simple, but delicious. We would skate the length of the canal, under the guise of seeing snow and ice sculptures, but all the while motivated by the tempting reward of a Beavertail. Another example: we went to Niagara almost every May long weekend. We would bike from Niagara Falls along the bike trail to Niagara-on-the-Lake, get some delicious homemade ice cream, and then bike back. Much like with dogs, a tired kid is a happy kid.

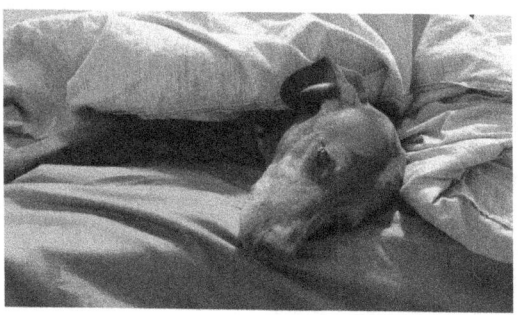

Photo Credit: Marcia Allyn Luke

We went to Orlando, Florida twice, once when I was three and once when I was 11. Both times we went to Disney World and both times were amazing. And there were many other places in between: Daytona, Florida; Charlotte, North Carolina; Talladega, Alabama, to name a few. Anyone notice a pattern? Yes, these cities are all home to a NASCAR racetrack. My parents loved going to the races and a couple of times we would go as well, but mostly we hung out with grandma while the grown ups went to the track.

Our journeys across Canada were much more wholesome. My mom would plan to visit every parliamentary building in every province. We saw every tourist destination we could on our way, including any statue of an enormous animal:

- the Wawa Goose,
- Husky the Muskie,
- the Shediac Lobster,
- Ogopogo (Canada's loch ness monster), and
- Restigouche Sam the Salmon.

There were other monuments as well, the Terry Fox monument in Thunder Bay, the Big Nickel in Sudbury, the Big Apple in Colborne, all of these in Ontario. She had us scheduled from morning to night and we were so exhausted that we went right to bed with no fuss. The grown ups would stay up playing euchre and drinking Canada Cooler Rockaberry by the two-litre bottle.

There were also many things I enjoyed about living in the country and one of these was having friends that lived on farms. In fact, our next-door neighbours lived on a farm just up the road and we would spend time there helping them during haying season, playing with baby animals, or using the rope swing in the barn. I was able to witness amazing things like cows giving birth, mating season (I know…), and spent a great deal of time horseback riding with one of my best friends. I would go to her house for the night and then end up staying the whole weekend. We would do the chores in the early morning before the sun had really come up. We would each grab one of the plaid jackets from the breezeway (they all smelled pleasantly like hay), so we didn't get our clothes messy or dirty.

And then we would come in for breakfast. Breakfast at my house was a whole host of sugary cereals: Frosted Flakes,

Cocoa Puffs, Froot Loops, or Captain Crunch. We were mostly on our own except maybe Sunday morning mom would make pancakes, French toast, or poached eggs on toast (one of my favourites). Breakfast on the farm was eggs, bacon, sausage, fruit, and stacks of buttered toast higher than I had ever seen before. When your job involves physical labour all day long, you need a great deal more food to fill the void.

Some weekends my best friend and I would ride horses all weekend, exploring their property and talking as we rode. On one of my first rides with her, the horse I rode (named Cindy) started to trot a little faster as we reached the end of her long farmhouse driveway. Then rounding the corner, she broke out into a full-on canter. I was holding on for dear life, exhilarated but also terrified, with my friend yelling urgently behind me. I thought she was just telling me to hang on. At the top of the driveway, we didn't stop though. We started heading for the barn…through the loading chute. The loading chute was higher up so not only was I going to be jumping Cindy for my first time (she had clearly done this before), but it also had a rail that ran along the middle of ceiling inside the barn and a big bucket to move hay down the aisles when feeding the animals. I finally realized that my friend was yelling "DUCK!", just as we jumped the loading chute and entered the barn. So, I crouched down hugging Cindy's neck and when we came to a stop, I slowly looked up to realize that my head would have been split wide open by the rail.

After one of my first sleepovers, I woke up and my leg was itchy. I noticed that I had little, red bumps in one spot on my leg. My friend smirked and said they were probably bites. "From what?" I asked, though I probably should have kept my mouth shut and called it a day. "Willard. The spider that lives in my room." Yet another experience that cemented in my heart a hatred for spiders. Another night, in an effort to convince me to like rap music, she played Salt 'n' Pepa's "Push It!" all night long on repeat. It was a lesson in how some things grow on you after a while.

Sometimes, if the weather wasn't good or the ground was too soft for the horses, we would sit and watch music videos on my best friend's satellite dish. This was a novelty since my parents still had an old TV antennae that got very few channels. I saw some videos that were probably quite inappropriate, but had fun. Then we would raid the kitchen coming up with our own meal concoctions. I think the best one, and worst, was pizza on toast. We would make toast, spread some spaghetti sauce on, add a slice of Kraft cheese, and, if we were lucky, some pepperoni or ham. Then we would put this in the microwave to melt the cheese. It was delicious and at the same time disgusting.

Another thing I loved about living in the country, was the ability to jump on my bike to go places. My other best friend lived just on the other side of the train tracks, so we would meet at the tracks and go to her house, or mine, to hang out. She loved reading and exploring the outdoors and playing games. I remember doing makeovers with her and throwing pretend concerts. We spent a significant amount of time talking about everything and nothing. We also ended up in Girl Guides together. We would go to meetings every week and then camp on the weekend several times a year together. It was amazing having a friend with whom I could share my love of the outdoors.

So, living in the country was great, until about the time that the teenage hormones kicked in. Then I started wanting to go to parties and stay late at school for extracurricular activities. From a parenting perspective, having to drive your kid everywhere is pure genius—you always know where they are! From a kid perspective, with parents that were extremely conservative about the teenage social scene, this was a complete nightmare.

As a result, I couldn't wait to go to university and there was never a question in my mind that I would go away to university. My dad wanted me to go to a local university so that I could live at home and drive back and forth to campus. From a financial perspective, it made complete sense. But about the same time that I hit puberty, my dad and I started to butt heads. In a big way. My dad is a car guy so he's very hands-on and never understood my love of school and books. My dad and my sister had much more in common. She didn't like school and had a handful of close friends, but didn't care much for the social scene. She was tame as far as teenagers go. In other words, she didn't break my parents in very well.

And then I came along with my nose in a book, loving school, and wanting to do anything and everything with my friends. My dad knew many people, but always said that you couldn't trust anyone. This made me sad and I was determined to prove him wrong. There were so many differences in our personalities that we just couldn't see eye-to-eye.

Parenting Perspective
Honesty is the best policy

I'm not sure what the exact formula is, but here's my take so far. Don't ever put your kids in a position where they would rather lie to you than tell the truth. Entertain all conversations. Don't get too distracted, don't roll your eyes, don't huff in frustration. Think about your response and the reasoning behind it before you deliver your answer. And come up with alternatives or have your kids come up with alternatives.

My parents did a good job in many ways, but where I think they failed in this respect was they sometimes reacted out of fear without any explanation and there was a marked lack of communication. There were expectations and rules, but no dialogue. I know already that I'm not the most patient person in the world, so this will require Herculean effort and there will be times that I lose my mind. But my hope is that I can at least enter into a conversation with my kids so that they understand why I was upset in the first place. Depending on how this philosophy works out for me, I may be backpedalling on this strategy in about 10 years.

Photo Credit: Brett Jordan from Pexels

Throw in a strict upbringing by his own parents and my dad's favourite saying on the weekend became, "you don't need to go!" Well, there are many things we don't need to do, but we like to do them. Eating three meals a day, for example. We even had scheduled 'stay home and be bored' weekends. On the calendar. In pen. Ugh.

This was the dynamic that developed as I saw it: unreasonable restrictions and a disconnected relationship with my dad. And so, I started to lie about where I was going. My parents didn't want me going to a party? Then I would just go to a friend's house for a 'sleepover'. Looking back on this, I realize my plans weren't necessarily the safest. And now, as a parent, I want to avoid my children lying to me at all costs. Especially because I know what that entails from the other side.

Life Lesson
Don't lie to your parents

If you feel like you have to lie, chances are you're doing the wrong thing (the same goes for hiding something). Maybe you screwed up and don't want to confess. It's always easier than having to face the music at some undetermined point in the future. Own it, tell the truth, and say you're sorry. Sometimes, you may have to initiate the difficult conversation. But it's always worth having. If you don't know where to start, ask a question. Not a "yes or no" question, but a "who, what, where, when, why, or how" question. If it's a conversation you can't have with your parents, have it with an aunt/uncle, a grandparent, or someone your parents trust.

Photo Credit: Miguel A. Padrinan from Pexels

I was a good kid. I didn't do drugs. I didn't get arrested. I wasn't a teenage pregnancy statistic. I was smart and responsible, when I wasn't lying. But because I lied to get what I wanted, there were many times that I wasn't where I was supposed to be, and the outcome could have been much worse.

For example, one of my friends lived in town and she had a party at her house, without parental supervision. Her mom was 'pretty cool' that way so she addressed any concerns the parents had, and the official plan was the boys would go home and the girls would sleepover. That night was my first time getting drunk, I walked in on one of my friends having sex, and I took off on my own late at night wandering the streets for a good portion of time (something that became a bit of a habit for me). I really have no idea how I found my way back to her house or where I slept, but I know it wasn't with a boy. The result was harmless, but how many ways could this scenario have gone wrong?

- One of the boys that was there could have decided taken advantage of me.
- I could have been accosted during my nighttime stroll.
- I could have ended up with alcohol poisoning or being drugged.

- I could have fallen down the stairs (for which I also developed somewhat of a habit, and not when I'm drunk).
- I could have decided to have sex that night and maybe become a teenage pregnancy statistic.
- The cops could have busted the party.

In this situation, my parents at least knew where I was, but can you imagine if I had also been somewhere else? WTF was I thinking? About hanging out with my friends.

Part of the appeal to going away to university became the freedom. And it wasn't irresponsible freedom that I sought. I needed that time away to figure out who I was outside of being my parents' kid and learn to correct my own compass when it went in the wrong direction.

Freedom also meant the urge to be close to people and things so that I didn't have to rely on my parents or their car. And so, began my fascination with living in the city. I associated both things together, school and the city, and to me it meant a more sophisticated life. I had learned all I could from living in the country. Now I wanted the exact opposite. I ran away from my roots and for a time forgot who I was.

Parenting Perspective
Do you know where your children are?

My parents did many things right. We went camping and had family gatherings, which created opportunities from a young age to bond as a family. Once my dad and I started fighting in my teen years, I think they lost me. At that point, my attachment to my friends became more important than almost anything else. It must be hard when your kids are full of hormones and you're doing what you can to guide them during a very tumultuous time. I feel strongly that real conversations and continued opportunities to bond would have helped prevent me from straying. What if my parents had asked me what I wanted to do with them? What if we went rock climbing as a family? Or to an amusement park? My mom often did these things with us, but my dad was often absent. My plan is to foster my kids' interests in addition to sharing my own. Include the friends that are good influences when possible. And even following disagreements, do what you must to repair the relationship with honesty and communication. That way you will not only know where your children are physically, but emotionally as well.

Photo Credit: Geralt from Pixabay

My dad had fixed up a car for my sister when she was 16 and so he did the same for me. They covered the insurance since it was cheap to add me onto their own, but I had to take care of it and put gas in the tank. It was a burgundy 1986 Oldsmobile Cutlass Supreme, V8 (my sister's first car was a teal green Camaro, by the way). It was a Grandpa car with a bench seat in the front. The material was velvet and burgundy. I named her Betsy[2]. Betsy had wheels, it was better than riding my bike, and she had more than a little pep. In fact, I remember getting stuck in an inch of snow. I would tap the gas pedal and the tires

---

[2] I have named all of my vehicles along the way: Betsy (1986 Oldsmobile Cutlass Supreme), Blue (1992 VW Passat), Madeleine (1993 VW Passat), Juanita (2000 VW Jetta), Lola (2010 Nissan Rogue), Beast (2009 GMC Acadia), Stella (2013 Jeep Grand Cherokee). The only one I don't remember naming was the 2017 GMC Silverado when we lived in Port Hope.

would just spin like crazy. My dad taught me how to wash the car carefully, check the oil and tire pressure, refill the washer fluid, and to call him if anything beyond that happened. He was and still is my tow truck service. And since I was responsible and had a car, I became the designated driver. I liked it because then I always knew I had a safe ride home. Some of my friends weren't as reliable and that made me nervous.

The summer before I went to university, I worked two jobs: a gas station and the fast-food restaurant across the street. I would finish my shift at one, change my uniform in the washroom, and walk across the street to the next. I worked hard and saved some money, and my excitement grew as the day approached. When my parents and I arrived at university, I saw a Guelph police car and realized that I was going to be living in a whole other city. Yes, that was the point, but it hadn't really hit me until then. I remember crying as my parents drove away and feeling rather lost. I guess that's what comes from your mom being your Brownie leader, delivering your hot lunches at school with the parent teacher association (PTA), and generally being around all the time. Or maybe it's growing up in the country. Or maybe it was just me. I was homesick for a good while before I came out of my shell.

When I went to Guelph for university, I had:

- Only ever been on a city bus once in my life.
- Lived in the same general area my whole life.
- Switched schools only once.
- Only been out to the bar once and it wasn't great.
- Travelled but never been on an airplane.
- A steady boyfriend.

At university, I did only what was required for the first two months. It was enough to figure out where my classes were and thankfully, I chose a campus that was self-contained. I ate in the cafeteria attached to my residence. I made microwave Kraft Dinner in the lounge microwave. And I didn't go out.

For all these reasons, my first-year roommate (assigned by the powers that be at the university) was perfect. She was outgoing, generous, and made friends easily. Our room became a social hub. I had a small portion of the room with my own door which suited me fine.

Life Lesson
Don't drink on an empty stomach

Eat something substantial for dinner, have plenty of water or Gatorade before you go to bed and even some Advil for good measure. A pre-bedtime snack isn't a bad idea, especially if it's carbohydrates. Leftover pizza will do well. And shower before you go to bed. Also, if you're going to do shots, have a glass of water per shot. And don't play drinking games. Ever. If you do and you're anything like me, expect to be throwing up for the following 24 to 36 hours. And it doesn't always happen at home; avoid losing your lunch in a bathroom like this...

Photo Credit: Free Photos from Pixabay

The outer door was always open and since she had a TV and cable there were many nights when 10 or so girls were piled on my roommate's bed or on the floor watching

Dawson's Creek or *Party of Five*. It allowed me to be social without having to do the work. And I could close my door if I wanted. It was perfect. I had refused all invitations to go out to the bar, but on Halloween my roommate wasn't taking no for an answer. I finally told her why I was reluctant—I didn't want to get left behind and I didn't know these girls that well. She assured me that we would all keep an eye on each other and no one would be left behind. And so, I dressed up in a French maid costume and went out for Halloween. We danced and had a great time, and it was the perfect night. Except that my parents were coming to visit the next day, I had only had a grilled cheese sandwich for dinner, and I had been drinking all night, rolling into bed at about two in the morning.

When my parents arrived, I was in the shower having thrown up all morning and finally gotten out of bed minutes before their arrival. My dad was tired from driving, so he laid down on my bed which probably reeked of booze and smoke (there was still smoking in bars then). My mom and I went down to the cafeteria to have breakfast/lunch and I was doing all I could to keep it down. After my first experience going out, I began to enjoy being away at school a great deal more.

Was I the perfect student? No. In fact, even for an excellent high-school student, university was still a bit of a shock academically. I managed to maintain a 75% average throughout, I worked to reduce the financial burden, I went home on a somewhat regular basis, and I had fun. I think I managed to find a good balance. Balance is key.

I loved living in Guelph and stayed for a few years even after graduating university. It was a city that felt like a small town. It had a vibrant downtown with lots of excellent restaurants. The downtown area had a wonderful community of like-minded people, who supported independent stores and services unfailingly. It was quite different from the nearest city I had growing up, and where most of my family lived, Oshawa. Oshawa was a blue-collar city dominated by General Motors (GM) workers. Oshawa favoured big box stores and the downtown was somewhat neglected and tired. Restaurants came and went quickly; tattoo parlours and convenience stores thrived. In many ways, Guelph was an excellent choice for my departure from the country. It was a city, but not too much city. When I finally returned home, I was surprised and impressed to see that Oshawa had changed. After GM suffered huge job losses and was eventually shut down, Oshawa welcomed a university alongside the already thriving college. Some of the campus buildings moved downtown and slowly others invested in businesses and restaurants too. Oshawa became much like the university town I knew and loved.

Following university, I got an internship at a magazine in North York. I was still living in Guelph but eager to get my career started. I felt ready for a change and a challenge. Part of the challenge was commuting from Guelph to North York for three months. There were times when I was in the car for five hours or more a day. I say "in the car" because I wasn't necessarily driving. The traffic was bonkers, and I remember on several occasions pounding the steering wheel and screaming at my windshield in frustration.

When the internship turned into a job three months later, naturally, I moved. This was my chance to live in the big city (or almost, North York was north of downtown Toronto), have a job that I'd always dreamed about, and make it bigtime. My commute to work went from five hours to five minutes. One of my friends from university also lived there which was fantastic. I was five minutes from Yorkdale mall, I could walk across the street to get groceries, and there were so many excellent restaurants to try. I even bought a new, professional-looking wardrobe.

> Life Lesson
>
> ## Know your limit, stay within it
>
> *Have you ever "bitten off more than you can chew?" or "ate so much you nearly split your pants?" Seeing what you want and knowing what you can handle is a fine art. It's not something you can figure out in your mind. It's something you know from past experiences of overdoing it. But it's also something that you can feel in your heart. When I toured campuses, Guelph felt right. I am the kind of person who likes to analyze and dissect everything in my brain, so I've had to learn (sometimes the hard way) that your heart knows better sometimes.*
>
>
>
> Photo Credit: Alexander Kovalyov from Pexels

Part of my job was writing for the magazine, managing freelancers, and copyediting. The other part of my job was account management for the advertising firm that published the magazine, so I drove all over the city exploring as I went from office to office. I learned so much during that year and a half and had a wonderful time. I was seriously considering buying a condo. But something just wasn't quite right. I began to stay at work later than necessary to avoid going home. I began to wear ear plugs at night just to sleep. I began to look forward to my sometimes weekend trips home more than was typical. I loved the magazine work, but began to dread the rest.

I was running regularly, eating clean, and going to the gym but wasn't happy. I felt stressed out as soon as I walked out the door in the morning. There was too much noise and too many people and everything was such a fast pace. I couldn't block it out. It was even too much for BUZZ BOM.

I started applying for jobs at publishers outside of Toronto and, as I'll explain in Chapters 2 and 3, eventually got a job in Whitby, Ontario. What this meant though was that I had a tough decision to make: stay in North York with my roommate at the time, get an apartment on my own close to my new job or move home with my parents and save for a house. Though keeping my independence was important, I decided that saving for a house was essential and moved home. I didn't necessarily realize until afterwards that I needed the peace and quiet of the country too. These are just a few of the things I've re-embraced from my youth that make me happy:

- The great outdoors, including camping trips.
- A place to walk the dog, preferably with trails.
- Country music.
- Bike riding.
- Bonfires.
- Long drives on country roads.
- Laying in a hammock looking up at the sky or listening to the wind in the trees.

My weekend visits had become almost like a trip to the cottage. There was no lake, but it felt like a cottage where you could rest and relax. It didn't matter what you wore, if you had your makeup done, or how much you slept. There was this outdoor bliss ready and waiting to soothe your soul. It was the beginning of my return to my country roots.

Chapter 2
Not too cool for school

Education is one of the best ways to open doors and open your mind. Seize any opportunity you can to learn something new, challenge yourself to think differently, or engage in critical thinking and dialogue. You only get one brain; education is the best way to cultivate and grow your brain power. And read books. Any and all books, no matter what the cover looks like.[3]

Photo Credit: Lil Foot from Pixabay

I've always loved school, but I know it doesn't come easily to everyone. My sister always struggled with

---

[3] Weinstein, Y., Sumeracki, M., & Caviglioli, O. (2018). *Understanding How We Learn: A Visual Guide* (1st ed.). Oxfordshire, England: Routledge.

school. She didn't like it and often found that she didn't fit into the prescribed box. She was incredibly good at demonstrating learning, but found tests challenging. I loved reading from a young age and was thrilled by the act of learning. I always wanted to please my teachers and was proud when I learned something new that I could share.

In grade four, we moved, and I started at a new school. There were many times that I would finish my work well before the other students. My teacher would send me down to one of the kindergarten classes and I would write, illustrate, and read books to the kindergarten students.

My elementary school from grade four to grade eight was excellent at providing enrichment opportunities. I remember getting on a bus, going to a different school, and meeting other students from all over the school board. Sometimes we would participate in critical-thinking and problem-solving activities by doing difficult puzzles and challenges. Sometimes it would be art or music. Sometimes it would be a writing workshop. We were still responsible for completing our regular schoolwork, but it prevented many of us from getting bored and maybe getting into trouble.

Parenting Perspective
Don't judge a book by its cover

Just because your child doesn't like school, doesn't mean they don't like anything about school. Or maybe they haven't found that one thing yet. Maybe you'll have to talk to the teacher to find the right fit. Kids are in school for a long time and often kids who are bored end up getting labelled as troublemakers. And if your child is getting good grades, that doesn't necessarily mean they aren't bored. Don't judge that book by its cover; try anything and everything.

Photo Credit: Towfiqu Barbhuiya

One of these enrichment programs was related to politics or public speaking. We took turns conducting and participating in interviews that were videotaped. Then we would watch the tape to make improvements to our presentation style. When I watched my video, I noticed that I was fidgeting the entire time. I was rubbing my hands together between my knees, which shifted my body and made me look like I was hunched over. I was horrified, but managed to do it again with minimal fidgeting. It was such a powerful learning experience in 'soft skills' like confidence, public speaking, and enunciation. The opportunity to correct my mistakes immediately was extremely effective.

Another program was an art program and we worked with pottery to create figurines. I couldn't for the life of me think of something to do, so I sat around wracking my brain and wasting all my time. I finally decided to do a dolphin, but had little time remaining. When I collected my dolphin from the kiln, I realized I had forgotten its dorsal fin. Once again, I was mortified. I realized that I was overthinking during the idea stage and that I should have picked something I was more familiar with, like a favourite animal or plant. I also learned to review my work before it's set in stone (pun intended, ha-ha!).

When I first went to high school, my mom 'volun-told' me to enroll in grade 10 drama. She felt that I was too reserved and wanted to encourage me to come out of my shell. It did the trick, sort of. At the end of the class, we played a game where we all had to imitate someone in the class (without using words) and one of my classmates sat in the corner with his arms around his knees. Everyone knew it was me. Sometimes it made me uncomfortable, but these are the experiences that help a person grow. In grade 11, I even became the assistant stage manager for a play, so something must have stuck. It helped that some of my friends were doing it too. I am an organized person by nature, so the role fit me well. I kept track of everyone and everything. The community of theatre was new and welcoming and appealed to my creative side. I ended up taking drama all the way through high school and even acted in a play in my final year. Acting forced me in many ways to get to know myself better so that I could play someone else. It made me look inside myself to dig up emotions and actions that I maybe didn't want to feel or remember.

In grade 12, I became convinced that I had to get on students' council to make it into a good university. Where I got this idea, I have no recollection. I put an extraordinary amount of stress on myself as a result. Thankfully, I did make it as fundraising coordinator. Not the position I applied for, but it didn't matter at that point. I felt at home with other people who were leaders, but was also intimidated by them. One of the biggest tasks for the fundraising coordinator was the chocolate campaign. Students would sign out boxes of chocolates and sell them, returning the profits so the student's council could host events for the student body. It was incredibly stressful keeping track of everything. I don't remember having many happy memories about my time on student council, but I was proud of my accomplishments. I met some great people, but chose not to do it again.

I had several favourite teachers in high school, but my OAC English teacher made the top of the list. For those of you who don't know, OAC stands for Ontario Academic Credit and was the equivalent of grade 13 in my day. They've since done away with OACs as well, but these credits were intended for students planning to go to university to bridge the academic gap between high school and post-secondary school. My OAC English teacher brought English literature to life in a way I hadn't experienced before. He uncovered hidden meanings and contextual significance. He taught us how to research the finer details so that we understood the author's message more fully. He had such a passion for the written word. His favourite book during the semester was *The Catcher in the Rye*. He had such a difficult time choosing the best part of the book that every time he would refer to a passage, he would say "this is my favourite part!" *The Catcher in the Rye*[4] has been one of my own favourites ever since.

Now to say that I felt like I belonged throughout elementary and secondary school would be a stretch. I had friends, but was never one of the cool kids. Much of my time was spent trying to go unnoticed. I always knew I wanted to go to university; it was never a question in my mind. When it came time to apply for school, I still didn't know what I wanted to do for work. So, I chose my favourite subject, English, and applied to complete my Bachelor of Arts.

I tried on many different hats throughout my educational career, trying to find my place. When I toured campuses though, it was clear to me which university I was attending. Guelph felt like home from the very beginning. As I mentioned before, I was still a nervous wreck leaving home but also extremely excited.

---

[4] Salinger, J. (1991). *The Catcher in the Rye* (1st ed.). Boston, MA: Little, Brown and Company.

Life Lesson
If at first you don't succeed, try, try again

Some people know exactly where they are supposed to be and when, what they want, and how they will get there. It's okay if you don't. Part of life is trying on different hats and seeing how they fit. This may take a while, your interests may change, or you may develop several interests that don't seem to fit together. Your heart will know when you have found something worthwhile.

Photo Credit: Vedanti from Pexels

My English classes housed many people just like me: book nerds. I took a variety of other classes trying to find a minor: anthropology, psychology, geography, drama, philosophy, political science, and criminal justice. I spent so much time taking different subjects to figure out my minor that I didn't end up with a minor. I didn't want to stay for an extra year to fulfill the number of credits required, so I stuck with my mish mash of subjects and called myself a 'well-rounded generalist'. I also experimented with my extracurricular activities. I went to a cheerleading tryout because they didn't have a gymnastics team. I considered student's council again. I was recruited by some friends to play recreation level volleyball and innertube water polo. I wrote for the school paper. I joined the rock-climbing gym. And in second year, I was a residence assistant.

I found more like-minded people in each of these activities. Sports were always the most difficult for me. I felt like (and was actually in many cases) the weakest link on the team, which made me extremely nervous, though everyone insisted it was just for fun. The only thing I stuck with throughout was rock climbing. There was no competition, except with myself, and it had more to do with your brain than your body in many ways. It was like solving a puzzle.

The University of Guelph was (and still is) full of many quirks:[5]

---

[5] The University of Guelph. (2021, February 5). About the University. Retrieved February 16, 2021, from https://www.uoguelph.ca/about/

- The Bull Ring: A circular brick building in the middle of campus, it was originally used to show bulls for the agricultural school but then turned into a pub, and then a cafe.
- Painting the Cannon named Old Jeremiah: We would get up at 4am with our housemates to spray paint an antique British naval gun and then head to class exhausted only to see that someone had painted over it at 5am.
- Aggie Pub: Hosted at different venues, the agricultural students would blow off steam and do the two-step. It's rather impressive if you've never seen it before; couples in cowboy hats and boots swirling around the dance floor in one gigantic circle. I never tried it because, well, I'm accident prone.
- The Arboretum: Guelph is full of many actual tree huggers and environmentalists. "This green space (that is connected to the main campus of the University) is over 400 acres of trees, gardens, trails, wetlands, and more".[6]

---

[6] E&L. (2020, July 28). 21 things to do in Guelph, Ontario (+ tips from a local). Retrieved February 16, 2021, from https://www.ontarioaway.com/things-to-do-in-guelph-ontario/

- War Memorial Hall: I only had one lecture here (the largest lecture hall on campus), but attended many movie showings in the evening! It's not uncommon to see people taking graduation photos outside of War Memorial Hall.

The University of Guelph has a beautiful campus, the kind where you would study on the grass at Johnston's green or witness wedding photos taken in front of the many historical buildings. The city itself is quite amazing and full of character. There is a town square with a fountain and it's the hub of the city. The residents of Guelph support independent businesses with unparalleled ferocity. And Guelph hosts some of the best music festivals in the province.

Throughout my university career, I worked in order to help pay for tuition and living expenses. I had an excellent job in the summer driving city buses in Oshawa, but I could always use a little more money and I didn't want to rely too heavily on the 'Bank of Mom and Dad'. I was a hostess at a restaurant for a couple of semesters, I was a residence assistant (for which you don't get paid, but your residence fees for the semester are waived), and I worked at the front desk in the athletic centre on campus. After university I still didn't know what I wanted to do, so I stayed in Guelph and worked a variety of jobs: selling memberships at a gym, teaching lessons at the rock-climbing facility in town, and stocking shelves at the independent bookstore downtown. The bookstore was a gem in Guelph, housing not only the bookstore, but a cinema, restaurant, and bar as well. I once again found my 'book nerds' and thoroughly enjoyed working there. One of the amazing things I had the opportunity to do at the bookstore was start a book club. This was right up my alley and I took it very seriously. I posted signage around the bookstore and people came every month. I would choose the book, do my research so I could facilitate discussion, and then we would meet in the bar upstairs. A wide variety of people would attend, and I felt the thrill of starting something successful. It reminded me of being back in English class, digging deep into a work of literature to uncover its secrets. From then on, I have tried to be part of a book club—it's certainly one of my loves in life.

Another of my loves is writing. I used to write poetry and short stories as a kid, and then when I wrote an article for the school paper, I knew I was hooked. It all started with a conversation. I was talking to my mom, telling her that my landlord owned almost 30 houses across the city with two other guys. She knew how much we were paying for rent and said, "that's criminal! You should tell someone about this...other people should know that they are gauging students!" This also coming from the woman who, on the way home from moving me in, cried from Guelph to Toronto because the house was such a dump. The quality of the house compared with the cost of rent was especially astonishing. I went to the student paper and told them my idea and with a little guidance from my mom, who had owned several houses at this point, I did some research. I called banks and the city, found out about mortgage rates and property tax, insurance, etc. We were paying for our own utility bills so that was covered. When I published the article, I determined that my landlord and his partners were making up to $140,000 each per year from student housing that was largely considered 'dumpy'. My story made the front page.

Years later, a unique and very intellectual project that I was honoured to work on was meant to help women break through the so-called 'glass ceiling'. My place of work initiated the group to support women's success in the workplace. It was open to men as well and we had a few men involved, both to benefit from the offerings and support their colleagues. I was asked to co-chair the organization and worked with some wonderful people. We had workshops on self-promotion, work-life balance, politics in the workplace—areas that were a challenge for many women. We had a book club (surprise, surprise) focused on professional development resources. And we had several partnerships within the community.

One of these was with the local college. They were planning to show a documentary called "Miss Representation" about women in the media. They were looking for partners and myself and my co-chair met with them. The plan was to have a panel after the screening to discuss the issue of women's rights and potential action items. I was asked to be on that panel as a successful businesswoman. I was shocked. It was one of the biggest privileges of my life. I was thrilled to able to contribute and raise awareness on such an important topic.

I've thought several times of graduate school, at first at the end of my undergrad and then at every major turn in my career. My first attempt was completing my Law School Admission Test (LSAT) and applying to law school after my Bachelor of Arts (BA). My scores weren't bad, neither were my grades, but it wasn't enough.

Life Lesson
Never stop learning

The moment you stop learning is the moment you start to become obsolete, narrow-minded, and judgemental. I honestly believe that it requires effort to keep learning. The brain is hard-wired to seek out information that confirms what you already believe. If we didn't actively try to change our own minds and the minds of others, we would have an incredibly sad world indeed. What's the best way to do this? Keep asking questions![7] In fact, when I began teaching in my late 30s (more about this below), I used to teach this very concept in my conspiracy theories course, which used conspiracy theories to engage in critical thinking. I would tell my students to seek out multiple, credible, and contrary sources of information in order to ensure objectivity. Then we would use logic, critical thinking, and argumentation to decipher the truth.

Photo Credit: Paseidon from Pixabay

I was tired of living the student life at that point and was eager for a bit of a break to figure out what I wanted to do. After completing my Publishing Certificate at the age of 26 (more on this in the next chapter), I thought seriously about doing a Master's degree in Creative Writing. It might help me with my career, but it really it was something that I wanted to do because I loved writing. It didn't seem practical to spend the time and money on something that may or may not be beneficial.

When I was 38, I left publishing and began to teach; suddenly my reason for graduate school made itself known. I needed to bridge the gap between publishing and education, so I applied for a Master of Professional Education. So here I am, at 41, going back to school after 14 years. As I said, I love school. My goal is to get full-time work at the college, but my graduate degree will also increase my credibility in a number of other areas, so I don't think I can go wrong. I could do training, I could

---

[7] Weinstein, Y., Sumeracki, M., & Caviglioli, O. (2018). *Understanding How We Learn: A Visual Guide* (1st ed.). Oxfordshire, England: Routledge.

write, I could consult. It comes down to the fact that I love to use and stretch my brain.

Chapter 3
If you love what you do, you'll never work a day in your life

My parents always told me to find a job that I love to do—you spend a great deal of time at work and if you hate it, you'll be miserable. My dad is an auto body worker and while he loved what he did, he hated the politics in his workplace. He shifted from having his own shop to a regular nine to five with benefits because of my sister and me. When my dad was in his shop, he was in his element. People would stop him at gas stations and parking lots and admire his custom work. I've said it before, and I will say it again—my dad is extremely creative and artistic.

Photo Credit: StockSnap from Pixabay

> *My mom didn't have the opportunity to go to college or university (though she would have loved it!) because…she got married. In those days, you didn't need to do both and in fact my grandpa basically told her that he would pay for one or the other. My mom was a stay-at-home mom for many years and I felt she was happy. She was incredibly involved with our school and extracurricular activities. She went back to work when I was 10, knowing that they would have two girls going to post-secondary school. She worked her way up from an office administration position to eventually become a Chartered Insurance Professional. She felt the stress of her job immensely though.*
>
> *I am immensely proud of my parents and the life they created for my sister and me. I took their advice to heart and found something that I loved to do.*

My first job, like many youngsters, was babysitting. If you want to get technical about it, my first paid job was sweeping my grandfather's garage for five bucks and a can of pop, usually Cream Soda or Grape Crush. When I was 11 or 12, I took a course with my best friend and I started babysitting. Sometimes I babysat my younger cousin. Much of the time I babysat for my Girl Guide leader, who had two children. I kept on babysitting until I went to university, if I could fit it into my schedule. It was a pretty good gig and I enjoyed being around kids. I guess that's one reason that I knew I wanted children of my own.

My sister had worked at the local gas station in 'town' (don't blink, you'll miss it!). But when she went off to college, they were left without help. It was a family-run operation and they lived in the house next door to the pumps. They would hire help to come and work for a couple of hours in the evening so they could have dinner as a family and also afternoons on the weekend. At first, when I inquired about taking her place, they felt I was too young. And maybe I was, I would only have been 15. The following summer I managed to get a job at a horse ranch, helping prep the horses for trail rides, making meals for the riders, cleaning the cottages for overnight guests. Sometimes I was invited on the rides and since I have a fondness for horses, I jumped at the chance. It only lasted the summer though and this time when I reached out at 16 years of age, I got my sister's old job (mentioned in the previous chapter).

It was challenging, especially at first. It wasn't just a gas station. Like many small towns, it was the hub of the village. It was a convenience/grocery store, video rental, post office, and coffee shop. This is where I learned to multitask. I also learned to work quickly and efficiently. There were regular customers, and they were kind, and sometimes inappropriate, but harmless. There were times when it was so busy that I would be running for the entire shift. And then I experienced the Ride for Sight, motorcyclists fighting blindness.[8] All the motorcyclists participating in the Ride for Sight would stop at the gas station because the owner was a biker as well.

Picture this: you hear them in the distance, a hundred or more motorcycles. Your heart starts to beat faster and you break out in a sweat. You try to formulate a strategy in your head, but it's useless. All you can do is start helping people and go as fast as you can. They land like a swarm of bees, some at the pumps, some in the parking lot, but they're everywhere. In the store getting coffee and smokes, chatting with the owner in the garage. It's overwhelming. And amazing.

---

[8] Ride for Sight: Motorcyclists Fighting Blindness...the great Canadian tradition continues! (n.d.). Retrieved February 16, 2021, from https://www.rideforsight.com/

Life Lesson

Doors open when you know someone; don't close them

The summer before I went away to university, I knew I would need more than the gas station to save up for school. They gave me more hours which was amazing and then a restaurant opened across the road. I went in to apply and thankfully, I knew someone who knew someone, and I got a job. It might feel like cheating to use a connection, but it's the way the world works and the sooner you start to network and accept support from others, the better off you'll be. It's not cheating, it's getting a leg up.

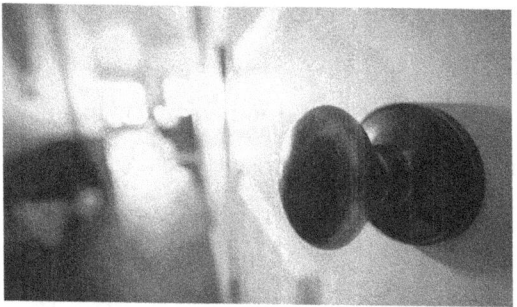

Photo Credit: Brett Sayles from Pexels

This group, for the most part, was jovial and patient. They weren't in a rush; this is a charity ride. They go easy on me, but what an experience. Then they all ride away as quickly as they arrive.

From my experience at the gas station, I learned how to deflect inappropriate comments with humour and sarcasm. I learned how to prove myself when I would have been underestimated. I learned the value of community from another perspective. I also mentioned before that for one summer I worked at the restaurant across the road from the gas station. At the restaurant, I learned about food prep and how to keep a restaurant clean. I learned about customer experience. I learned that some people aren't efficient or hardworking and sometimes you have to pick up the slack. The restaurant was the first of its kind in the town, so opening day was a big deal. All the successful and prominent members of the community came to support the opening. The restaurant had a drive-thru which was such a novelty. The regulars in town made it fun though. They would pull into the drive-thru at the restaurant and when they heard it was me, they would say "fill it up with regular." Jokes.

Fast forward from August to February, after I started my first year at university. I got a job as a hostess at a local restaurant to help supplement my meager savings. Then I received a phone call from my dad. The same dad that taught me to drive. The same dad that felt I was hopeless and bought me a huge grandpa car "so that there would be more metal around me when I crashed." The phone call went something like this:

"Have you figured out a summer job yet?"

"No, Dad. It's February."

"What do you think about driving bus?"

"What?!"

"You would start at 18 dollars an hour."

"Okay."

It turns out that the transit depot he worked at fixing buses hired students in the summer to cover for vacation time. They would hire anyone who could pass the training, but since most people didn't know about the summer program it was mostly employees' kids. It was the most amount of money I could make at the time, except for the General Motors factory which also hired students. But you most certainly needed a family member to get in there. Needless to say, I was incredibly nervous.

All the training was done by the depot; I basically had a personal mentor. There were so many videos to watch which were boring in the extreme. Two weeks of training in the office to pass the test and then two weeks of road training with other drivers to learn the practical ins and outs. When I took the bus on the road for the first time with my trainer, I was crawling at 30 kilometres an hour. He said, "let's take it up to the speed limit, alright?" I got the hang of maneuvering the bus and then I started learning routes. Keep in mind that I was five foot, five inches tall, and about 120 pounds driving a 40-foot bus. I was not exactly what most people expected when they stepped on my bus.

Now, part of my dad's concern with me driving was my coordination and attention. Remember "slow down!" Well, it was followed frequently by "watch where you're going!" The other part of his concern was my directional sense. When I was young, sometimes we would go to a restaurant as a family. On my way back from the bathroom, I would often get lost trying to find our table again. To say that this job was challenging every natural defect in my skillset thus far was an understatement.

> Parenting Perspective
>
> ## Help your kids out, but make sure they bust their butt
>
> *My parents were always willing to help me out financially and, in fact, made some big sacrifices to do so. But if it was something, I wanted then I had to bust my ass too. If I wasn't willing to work for it, then why should they pay the bill? I never had to pay rent as long as I was working or attending school, or both. I moved back home when I was in my mid-20s to save for a house and they had no issue with that either. Their goal was to help me get ahead, but not at the expense of learning to do things for myself.*
>
>
>
> Photo Credit: Breakingpic from Pexels

For the whole first summer, I drove the bus with the route map and schedule tucked under my leg on the seat…just in case. I even did it for the beginning of the second summer, afraid that I had forgot. When I finally felt comfortable with the routes, I then had to learn directions. For example, when someone calls on the radio asking for the "King West", I would have no idea if they were asking for me or not. I knew I was the King, but I would wait to see if anyone else answered so that I didn't get it wrong. Eventually, I learned by landmarks which one I was: heading to the mall was westbound and away from the mall was eastbound, for that route. Then I started to understand the map and which roads were north/south and which were east/west. This took time, but mostly it was just a matter of experience.

There was one time that an accident happened downtown and my dad was asking me about it after work one day. I told him it was on the southeast corner. He said it was the northeast corner and I thought about it again and said, "no, it was the southeast corner." Later that day or the next, he said, "you were right, it was the southeast corner" and I did a happy dance. Inside of course, but I felt like I had finally overcome my directional difficulties (at the age of 20), not without some serious effort.

There was another challenge to this job though. The passengers. This was a public-facing job and as much as I had done customer service before, I had never experienced anything like this. The (stupid) questions, the frustration (outright anger) when someone missed their transfer through no fault of my own, dealing with traffic (ignorant drivers), and then there were the young woman stereotypes (slander). I have stories, so many stories. I learned from this experience that me and the general pubic were not a good mix. I was feisty and my sense of truth and justice led me to be very frustrated with this job.

My perfectionism made me feel bad every time I ran late or had a less than perfect shift (which was always). But the money was good, and it paid for my post-secondary schooling, to a large extent. I was even able to come back during the winter holiday some years when I had enough seniority. In between summer and winter breaks, I would hostess, or work at the athletic centre to help supplement my funds and come about February, I would have to call the Bank of Mom and Dad for money.

I mentioned before that I struggled to figure out what I wanted to do for a career. I was always jealous of my sister because she never had a question in her mind. From an early age, I would say 15 or 16, she knew she wanted to be a paramedic. She didn't always have an easy time getting there, so she had her own challenges, but she always knew. In fact, when my sister found out that she had Crohn's disease, that also meant that she couldn't donate blood. As a future paramedic, she was devastated. I remember seeing her reaction and vowing to myself that when I was old enough, I would always donate blood because she couldn't. When I tell this story, it's not because I want people to think well of me. It's because I want people to know how much I love my sister.

After university, I worked several jobs based on the work I had already done to date and found little to no satisfaction. Then I had a conversation with a friend. I don't remember which of us asked the question, but it was something like this: "if you didn't have to worry about money, what would you do with your time?" This struck me as an excellent way to find my passion. What would I do? I would read books, write (but everyone knows you can't make money doing that), go to school forever, and at the time I would proofread my friends' papers and assignments. So, I thought, I will be an editor.

At the age of 23, I started looking at all my schoolbooks and applying to be an editor at various publishers. One of these publishers was kind enough to provide feedback when they sent me a rejection. They said that the individuals they were hiring had a degree or diploma in publishing. This was something I hadn't heard of, so I started doing some research. I found a program that I could do entirely online while I was working at the bookstore. I only had to go to campus twice: to register and to pick up my certificate. This program also offered internships, so that was a bonus.

Once again, I busted my ass, but I loved the program and felt strongly that I was on the right track. As I mentioned before, I managed to get an internship at a new homes' magazine in North York. It was a free magazine that was offered by an advertising agency and I was their Editorial Assistant. I helped to hire and manage freelancers, I wrote articles myself, I proofread and worked with designers. It was fabulous. Extraordinarily little money, but excellent experience.

When I was finished my three months, they wanted to hire me, but didn't have enough hours. So, I spent half my time with the magazine and half my time as an account manager for the advertising company. Their accounts were primarily new home builders, condos, townhomes, etc. I learned an awful lot about floorplans and building code, and the interesting characters that worked in the industry. I drove all around Toronto to different offices, learning my way around the city and how to maneuver it effectively using actual maps, not Google Maps. The best defense is a good offense in Toronto. It was a period of growth for me yet again. I bought professional clothes, even a suit, and felt like I had made it. I moved to an apartment in North York because the commute from Guelph was killer. I had a roommate and we lived on the 20th floor. It was pretty cool.

I learned that I loved publishing, writing, and editing. I enjoyed the work and the people, but eventually living in North York got to me. It was busy from the moment you walked out the door in the morning until you got home and closed your door at night. I'm glad for the experience and I certainly had fun while I was there. I wasn't making very much money though and I even considered going back to driving bus for a time. And then at the age of 25, I went to a life-changing Halloween party, a different Halloween party from the memorable one in first year university. There seems to be a pattern of life-changing events happening on or around Halloween: the beginning of a working relationship with a close friend (Oct. 2015); my first published book (Oct. 2019); certified for Irlen

Screening (Sept. 2020) and completed my first Irlen screening (Oct. 2020) (more about this in chapter six).

One of my best friends to this day, hosted a Halloween party and I went, thank goodness. I reconnected with some people I hadn't seen for an awfully long time. One of these individuals was working for an educational publishing company in the accounting department. When she heard what I was doing, she asked if I would ever be interested in working there. I was like "absolutely!" Of all the courses I took in the publishing program and all the different types of publishing that exist, educational publishing appealed to me because I loved school so much. It took a couple of tries, but I got a job as an editor and made the difficult decision to move home and save for a house. I was elated.

I was so glad that I didn't go back to driving a city bus just for a little money. I found my 'book nerds' again and I loved publishing. I worked for two and a half years as a developmental editor, working mostly on marketing and accounting textbooks. I decided that I wanted to become an acquisitions editor, so I took a sales role as a steppingstone for almost two years.

Life Lesson
Ask the tough questions

As a sales representative, one course will always haunt me. I had a good working relationship with the chair of the department, and they were using my book for the introductory course. They were extremely happy with me as a rep because I provided excellent service and knew the products well, but the chair was looking to leave her mark. She wanted to shake things up and she did. Partway through the process of selling her the new edition of our book, my Spidey sense started tingling. I felt that she wasn't being honest with me and I remember that moment well. I had asked her all the right questions and taken all the right steps, so I didn't feel I had the right to question her further. I should have and I regret that every day. She might have lied directly to my face anyhow, but I will never know. She did choose another company and even though I did everything I could, I was still disappointed. I did take some satisfaction from the fact that, after I left sales, they ended up using our textbook again. Ask the tough questions and learn how to do it early on. You don't have to be rude about it, but be direct.

Photo Credit: TeroVesalainen from Pixabay

I liked sales better than I thought. Once again, I was travelling around Toronto. I would get up ridiculously early and drive to beat the traffic and then sleep in my car for 45 minutes in the parking garage (a trick I learned while driving bus at all hours of the day and night).

I knew a great deal about the process of developing textbooks and the level of quality. I used what I knew to help me 'sell', even though most of the time I just felt like I was helping them find the right resources. Sometimes I had the right book and sometimes I didn't, but I kept working away doing what I could do and, low and behold, I made my number. It was a great feeling, knowing that I was helping to contribute to the greater good of higher education.

I remember having this exact conversation with one of my fellow sales reps on a bench on campus one day. What could be better than helping to educate young minds? I don't think she had ever thought of it that way before. I was passionate, I was good at organizing myself, I was good at answering questions and inspiring confidence in the company, and I was good at customer service and follow up. I learned how to present to large committees and I learned to ask the tough questions. I did move from sales to acquisitions and I think that was my favourite role in publishing, by far. Here's what I am good at:

- Writing & editing
- Reading & synthesizing
- Research & analytics
- Problem-solving
- Creativity
- Efficiency
- Project management

What do these skills translate into for me? A process of researching, coming up with solutions to problems, writing summaries and reports, initiating and mobilizing creative ideas, finding efficiencies, and managing the whole project from start to finish. That's not to say that I can do it all myself, but I have the big picture vision to steer the project in the right direction. And I have the autonomy to make decisions and do what I do best without being micromanaged. I was immensely proud of my accomplishments in acquisitions and I stayed for over four years.

So, if it was my favourite role to date, what happened? Why did I leave? I had signed a bunch of new projects in social sciences, but the direction of the company changed. It was purchased by an investment firm and they decided not to explore new markets. So, I had to kill many of the projects I had signed and fire the authors I had just hired. It was heartbreaking. This new direction continued for quite some time after I left. It eventually shifted again, but it squashed my spirit. I was 33 when I started trying to get into mainstream publishing, the kind that fills the shelves at bookstores. And then I got pregnant. I took extra time off because I wasn't ready to go back after a year. Then I started slow, with some freelance consulting and editing work part time. I enjoyed it, but it wasn't going to pay all the bills, so I got a job back at my former employer and the girls started daycare when they were 18 months old.

Life Lesson
Don't give up

This time I did some coaching with a mentor of mine and we concluded that teaching might be a good fit for me. I really enjoyed preparing and delivering training sessions at sales meetings, which was in many ways like teaching. Let me be clear: teaching adults, not children. So, I started reaching out to everyone I knew at a university or college, including authors I had worked with in the past. I searched LinkedIn for and connected with the head of the communications or business departments at every local college I could and asked them if they were hiring contract faculty. I pestered people until I got a yes or a no. When I had three courses secured for fall, I did a happy dance, and I gave my notice. This was the next frontier for me.

Photo Credit (adapted): James Wheeler from Pexels

Most moms I talked to said what they loved most about going back to work was talking to adults. For me, it was the feeling of being productive, having a purpose, and accomplishing things. I knew enough about the job and the role that my return to work went well, for awhile, but it soon became clear to me that it was the 'same old, same old'.

At age 38, when I shifted gears to teach, I only ever intended to teach online. With my knowledge of post-secondary educational technology, it was a no brainer. There are courses on a particular topic and then a number of sections offered on that topic to accommodate the large quantity of students. There are usually between 35 and 50 students per section. All the sections I secured were in person; I had two sections of Professional Writing and one section of Introductory Communications, at two different colleges. Teaching in person really wasn't any different from the sessions I ran at sales meetings in the past, but it also wasn't what I expected. It ended up being so much better. I had the opportunity to share my passion for reading and writing with students who didn't want to read and write. They were forced to take mandatory communications or writing by the college, and they thought they didn't need the help.

Parenting Perspective
Look at the kid that's in front of you

Much like teaching, you need to look at the kid that's in front of you. This is somewhat more difficult for parents. You have a history with your children, you have preconceived notions of what they should be, what you want for them. As a teacher, I am more objective, and I spend a relatively short amount of time with each student. For parents though, it requires constantly re-evaluating your own children as they change and evolve. And re-evaluating yourself and your own responses toward them. I will need to remind myself of this as I move through the journey of parenting as well. I truly feel that if you are looking (really looking) at the kid that's in front of you, you will be able to engage, communicate, and reach them in a much deeper way and they will engage, communicate, and reach back.

Photo Credit: Porapak Apichodilok from Pexels

It was a challenge and I love a good challenge. How was I going to get through to these students? How was I going to gain their trust and help them improve their skills? I told it to them straight, "I know you don't want to be here and maybe you don't think you need help. That's fine, but I can help you to improve your writing and communication, if you will let me."

I also gave them opportunities to write about things they were interested in while writing in a format or practicing a skill that would challenge them. For example, let's practice editing…on celebrity Twitter posts or let's practice being more concise and finding the key message by summarizing a page from *Harry Potter*. Yes, I still made them write about academic topics and conduct proper research. But by gaining their interest on these smaller tasks, it gave them the confidence to practice the skills when it came to the larger assignments. One of my favourites was analyzing tone and audience. I asked them to respond to a prompt and then we analyzed the text. What made it appropriate for an academic setting, for their professor to read? What parts of speech could they identify? Then I had them write it as a text message, social media post, news headline, or email to their boss. What parts of speech and language change? So much fun…for me at least!

And so, I taught for three years and loved it, trying to improve each semester and challenge my students in different ways. The most rewarding part is having a student come to you and say, "I never knew I could write like this, thank you so much! I am really enjoying your course…I've learned so much in your course that I never learned before." The most challenging sections were the skilled trades students. In some ways, they were easier because they recognized that they could improve, but they also didn't see the relevance. Why would they need to be a good writer to work in the trades? So, I showed them how good writing is good communicating and they need to communicate with clients all day long. How are they going to show they are different from others? How are they going to inspire confidence to get the job? I used my own experience with home improvements and hiring people to come into my own home. What made the difference? Why did I hire them? What would make me hire them again, or not?

They quickly saw that this could benefit them, and I tailored their assignments and activities as much as possible to make sure they saw the relevance. It was like a puzzle and every class was different. What tone should I use to communicate with them? How would I build trust? How far could I push them, and how fast, without losing them? What would be most useful for them during the rest of their academic career or in the workplace? Ultimately, I felt like I made a huge difference for many students. Did I lose some? Of course, but I took pleasure in the fact that it wasn't only the highly academic students that I helped.

During my time teaching, I received a wonderful opportunity. A friend of mine had been invited to author a chapter in a book about infertility and child loss (more about this later). She recommended me for the project as well, which was extremely exciting. I always wanted to write, but knew that it wasn't likely to pay the bills. I enjoyed my career in publishing, but still had that drive to become an author. I spoke with the editor and started writing my chapter. It was hard to believe that this opportunity fell into my lap so easily. That being said, I was turning 40 soon and felt the timing was meaningful. I wrote my chapter in the summer, turned 40 in September, and the book published in October. It made it to #1 on Amazon in two categories and #2 in another and it was labelled a 'Hot New Release' and 'International Bestseller'. It happened quickly and not without effort, but I was a published author! Sure, I had written articles for magazines or student newspapers, but I had never been published in a book. A real book. It was like a switch flipped for me. Now I had some street cred in the author world. The publisher was looking for contributors who were interested in working with her again and I told her I was interested. She never followed up, which is okay because it happened this way for a reason.

Fast forward a few months and I was talking with the same friend who had also contributed a chapter in the book. She asked me, "would you publish with them again?" I thought to myself, "with my publishing background, I would rather self-publish, and I think I could, now that I have my first one under my belt." My first book was a wonderful experience and I appreciated being a part of the project so very much. The final product is amazing and I met an incredible group of women. But I like to do things myself; my parents would attest to that fact.

I don't like to get stale, I enjoy learning and challenging myself and so I usually have something new going on, I'm generally working on several projects at once, and I sometimes struggle with work/life balance. But I love what I do and if I don't, then I change what I'm doing. If you love what you do, you'll never work a day in your life.

Chapter 4
A penny saved is a penny earned

Money won't buy you happiness, but it certainly goes a long way. You need to make ends meet and what does that even mean? It means you need to make enough money to live. Your basic human needs for food and shelter (electricity, heat, water) need to be met. The rest is, more or less, optional: TV, cell phone, internet, entertainment, eating out. Whatever you spend, you need to make; it's all about balance.

Photo Credit: Skitterphoto from Pexels

I mentioned that my first real money-making endeavours were sweeping my grandpa's garage and babysitting. I also received allowance for doing chores around the house. I didn't have any expenses, so this was just spending money for candy at the corner store. I remember my bedroom being the hottest in the house, something about the way the sun shone through the window. I branded my room 'Canary Island', made up signage, and started charging people to enter. It was probably cute at first, but soon became annoying to my family. Canary Island was my first attempt at entrepreneurship.

When I first started working at the gas station, I would ride my bike there and dad would pick me up when I was finished. The expense part of the equation didn't come until I had to put gas in my car. Most of my friends didn't have cars, they would simply borrow their parents' car or rely on their parents to drive them places. Since we lived in the country, my parents were sick of driving us around and my dad was a car guy, so we were luckier than most. My dad would find a wreck that he could fix up and put on the road. There wasn't really a question of having a car; it meant freedom for my parents as well as my sister and me. It was a wonderful step toward independence, but also responsibility. Now I saw how far my hard-earned money would go: filling the gas tank of a classic car with a V8 engine? Not far.

Parenting Perspective
To get a little, you have to give a little

The best thing that ever happened for my relationship with my dad, was getting a job. I'm certain he had some idea about the potential benefits. It wasn't an option, just "go and get a job". I didn't mind because what else was I doing? Just hanging out at home and it wasn't that I was opposed to work. It was a challenge. It helped me to understand the value of money in a different way. You learn how hard you have to work, for how much money you receive at the end of a day.

Photo Credit: Marcia Allyn Luke

If my dad and I weren't on the same page before, working brought us a little closer. We were maybe in the same chapter. I understood some of the life lessons he was trying to impart and I think he respected me a little more.

It gave us something to talk about that was interesting and constructive. And it kept me out of his hair.

From my perspective, it seemed that my parents always had money, but were good with it as well. They could buy what they wanted, but they were responsible enough not to overburden themselves financially. By the time I was 17, we each had a car (not brand new of course), my parents had a large home on two acres of land and a fifth wheel RV (recreational vehicle). My dad's vehicle was the only one that was brand new: a truck which he used to pull the RV. The truck was his baby.

By the time I started applying to universities, I had a solid grasp on the give and take of money. The 'give and take' of university was this: 1) go to a local university, save money by living at home, and keep my car, or 2) go away, incur living expenses, but give up the car. It was an exchange I would have seen as unfair earlier in life. How can they take away something I've grown accustomed to? My sister went away and got to take her car, it's not fair! My sister went to college for one year and rented a room in a house with a family. Her full-year college tuition was probably the equivalent of one semester of university. And she paid for most of it herself. I began to see that my four years of university tuition and living expenses was not insignificant. And I did bust my butt to pay for as much as I could, but I accepted the terms as they were presented because they made practical financial sense.

When I graduated, I still wasn't sure what I wanted to do with my life and career. I knew that I enjoyed my freedom and that I needed to figure things out on my own. I had a boyfriend at the time who was staying in Guelph and we decided to live together. My dad was not happy with this decision. He felt that I should come home, drive city buses full time, and save money until I figured it out. That would have been a good option for sure, but it was a stressful job and it definitely wasn't what I wanted to do long term. How would I ever figure it out working a job I hated? And giving up my independence at that point was out of the question for me. I worked a string of jobs that I didn't enjoy, but paid the bills. And it helped me to narrow down my path through the process of elimination. The jobs that I was interested in I wasn't qualified for, so I went back to school, part-time while I worked. I remember going downtown Toronto with my mom to register. My mom was always supremely supportive when it came to education. To her, the money was always worth the investment.

Life Lesson
It pays to take good care of your belongings

I used to think it was a bit over the top the way my dad treated his trucks, and maybe it was. He would buy a new truck and then trade it in within five years, which most people would consider to be throwing money away. You lose so much just driving it off the lot! The difference was that my dad took such good care of his vehicles that the trade-in value was significant. I had many friends whose parents would simply run a vehicle into the ground and then start over. Maybe they had the vehicle for a longer period, but they also sunk money into repairs keeping it alive for as long as possible. I saw the benefit of my dad's approach.

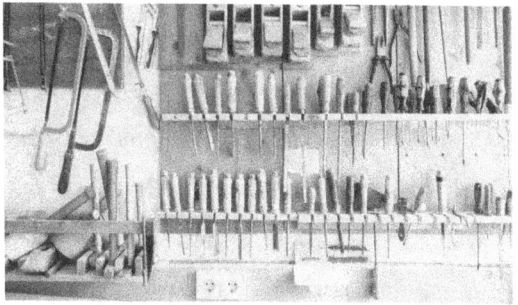

Photo Credit: Free Photos from Pixabay

At this point, my boyfriend was making decent money and helped me out by loaning me some money for school. I hated owing people money, but it was an incredible gift to have the help. The internship cost me more money than I made—there was a $1,000 honorarium for three months of work, but I was driving back and forth from Guelph to North York. I loved what I was doing though and again, the investment (or sacrifice) was worth it. I ended up getting a job and making okay money, but the expense of living in Toronto was horrific. So again, the question of balance came into play. I still didn't have much money and I still owed my boyfriend for school expenses, but I was staying afloat and getting real career experience. When I did finally get the job that officially began my career, the first thing I did was pay him back.

My first career job was close to home and I saw the fruitlessness of renting, which meant that I did sacrifice my freedom this time and moved home temporarily to save for a house. Again, not ideal, but it was getting me where I wanted to go. You have to start somewhere and work your way up. My grandmother had worked off and on throughout her life, but had been largely financially dependent on her husband. So, my grandma thought that the level of independence I wanted to achieve was not only smart, but impressive. I felt a connection with my grandmother during this time that transcended generational differences. It was almost like she was a wise, very loving older sister.

Saving for a house was my goal; why pay someone else's mortgage when I could be paying my own and building equity. Equity is one of those words as a kid that you don't understand at all. Once I did though, it was all I could think about. Luckily, my parents had a rule that as long as I was working or going to school, I could stay at home without being charged rent. They knew I had a purpose for coming home and they were happy to support something that made good practical and financial sense. It wasn't easy, but it also wasn't as difficult as I expected. Like my relationship with my grandmother, my relationship with my parents had changed too. My mom got on board early with me living my own life away at university and in her mind, nothing had changed with my move home. But my dad felt somehow that the old rules would still apply. My mom often played the role of mediator and reminded him regularly that his approach wasn't fair resulting in the establishment of new rules. For myself, having had roommates throughout university and recently in North York, I had learned to be a respectful roommate. I still didn't have complete freedom, but my parents respected the fact that I had been living on my own and I respected that they were letting me live in their house.

I had a solid understanding of the new home buying situation from my time working at the magazine. I knew that all condos would have condo fees and some townhomes too. Don't get me wrong, it's not that condos are bad. They serve a purpose for those who can't or don't want to worry about property maintenance. My goal was to find a freehold townhouse in my price range so I could avoid condo fees. It would be more affordable for someone just starting a career, and I was more than able to care for a property. But when I started looking at houses, I was somewhat discouraged. I was astonished at how much townhouses were and how much I would need to save for a down payment. Ideally, you want 25% down, but that's nearly impossible for your first home. So, I was aiming for 10%. (If you can achieve 25% down then you don't need mortgage insurance.) I was still saving my 10% down payment when I met someone. We were together almost a year before we moved in together. Buying a house with a partner is so much easier, not only to afford the down payment, but to carry the mortgage and expenses. Together, you are typically approved for a more expensive home and while I didn't want to be house poor, it was a relief.

That first house purchase was exciting and nerve wracking. They say your first house purchase is the easiest because you don't have a home to list, show, and sell. You also don't have to pay the real estate fees because the seller's agent pays for these. I would eventually learn from personal experience that they were right. The first house was in many ways my favourite house. It was a well cared for home built in 1969 with French doors throughout the main floor, crown moulding, and an amazing backyard with a huge maple tree. It had character. It was in an established and mature neighbourhood. We did some work on the house, but really that was minimal. The biggest project was building a deck in the backyard to create an outdoor oasis. We stayed there for eight years.

Within the first six months we quickly learned how additional costs can add up:

- The neighbour to the back decided to cut down the hedge separating the properties, so we decided to build a fence.

- The furnace had a crack in the heat exchanger so…new furnace.
- Furnishing a home and filling the gaps in our pooled resources. As much as we did things on the cheap, it's not easy, even on two incomes.
- There were also optional renovations along the way like hardwood flooring, light fixtures, and doorknobs.

Throw in an engagement ring, a destination wedding, a set of his and her dogs, and then, when I turned 31, we started trying to have a family. It wasn't as easy as we thought it would be and after three years, we decided to give the fertility clinic a try (more about this later). This meant that we were back to scrimping and saving. The costs went on our line of credit which we had used several times before for home renos, but always smaller amounts and then it would be paid off before moving on to the next project. We were lucky that every year, we would usually each get a bonus and combined with a tax return we would be in good shape again. The fertility clinic set us back about $18,000 though. This was different, it was huge. And then, if successful, would be followed by a maternity leave during which I would make next to nothing. We had to have it paid off before then. And we did.

Then the girls were born, and we started to think about what our future in that house would look like. Two girls who would eventually be teenagers and only one full bathroom? That sounded like a disaster. The options were to add a bathroom in the basement or to start looking at other houses. Around the same time, my mom was looking for an apartment (for reasons I will explain later). We talked with her about getting a house with an in-law suite and pooling our resources. She was helping quite often with the girls and didn't necessarily want to live alone, so we started house hunting again.

Each time we looked for houses we pushed what we considered our limit financially, though the bank likely would have given us more. This time we still purchased a resale house, but this one had a full basement apartment for my mom, four bedrooms, two full bathrooms, a double car garage, and backed onto a ravine. A great deal happened in this home even though we were only there for two years: most of my maternity leave, the girls' first trip (which was to Dublin, Ireland), the start of my freelance business, and eventually my return to work. This might have been our forever home, except that a builder was coming in to build apartments and townhouses across the ravine and there would be construction for 10 years.

They would also clear out a wide path in the ravine, increasing foot traffic and diminishing our privacy.

While this was a huge deal breaker there were also other things going on at the time. I was dealing with postpartum depression and I ended up suffering from a severe concussion at this house while renovating the backyard. It was an exceedingly difficult time for me. The new development across the ravine was a good excuse to try and find my ideal home which was always a spot in the country.

We did well selling our second house. In two years, the property value had increased by 50 per cent. Once again, we found a house that pushed our budget just a bit, but the equity we had built made it possible. If the first two houses were great, this one was paradise. It was a home originally built in 1840 just on the outskirts of a small town and it had four acres. It was oozing with character. The plan was to use some of the additional space to start a bed and breakfast which would help supplement our incomes. I mentioned teaching before…it was during this time that I decided to embark on the career change from publishing to post-secondary teaching.

Parenting Perspective
Do things with your kids, not for them

The first thing we had to do at our second house was put up a fence to keep the dogs contained. It was challenging to work around the trees and build it on a slope into the ravine, but thanks to my dad it turned out amazing. He was an integral part in teaching me about home renos. His creative side came into play often and we found another level to our father-daughter relationship. For the sides of the house, we did a regular wood fence for privacy, like you would see in any subdivision. Halfway down the side of the yard we switched to farm fencing so that we could still benefit from the green space. We renovated the deck as well and did some flooring, all of which we did ourselves, saving us a tonne of money. You could say that we liked to leave our mark on our houses. It was wonderful.

Photo Credit: Ivan Samkov from Pexels

Teaching would allow me the flexibility to run the bed and breakfast and still do some freelance work on the side. I was also overseeing some renovations to get the bed and breakfast ready.

The main floor washroom in the 1840 house was originally a laundry room with a farm sink and a toilet. It needed a tub or tub/shower combo, and as a result the laundry moved downstairs, in the scary fieldstone basement that looks like it's from the movie *Silence of the Lambs*. But it made the bed and breakfast suite possible.

The upstairs washroom was also showerless, so it needed a half renovation, and the third washroom had a sketchy stand-up vinyl shower that didn't even go up to the ceiling. So, three partial bathroom renos in the first few months.

Then within the first six months every appliance in the house died: the dishwasher never worked from day one, the fridge was next, then the air conditioner which was accompanied by the furnace, the hot water heater needed an upgrade, and the washer and dryer died. The only appliances that went the distance were the gas stove and fireplace, the hood fan, and the sump pump.

> ## Life Lesson
> ## Sometimes keeping busy is a distraction
>
> *This whole time I was focused on the renovations and my new teaching career. Once I had a moment to breathe, I realized that my paradise had turned into a prison. I had literally changed everything in my life: my job, my environment, my postpartum was under control, I was recovering reasonably well from the concussion, and I had a regular dose of nature every day. But I was miserable. My husband and I had never been further apart; the isolation of being in the country had placed a magnifying glass on our relationship, which I realized was broken.*
>
>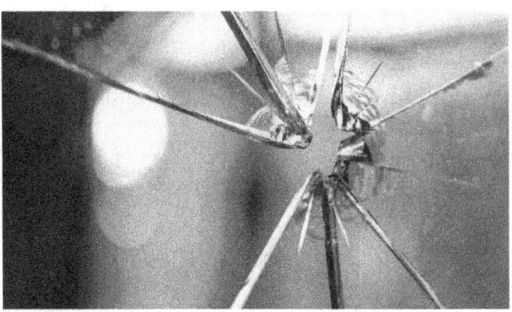
>
> Photo Credit: Kiragrafie from Pixabay

Since it was an older home, the fieldstone basement was letting out a significant amount of heat between the stone and the beams. I hired a spray foam company to come in and spray the headers. The fieldstone was in good shape which was a relief. Being in the country, we wanted to be able to hook up to a generator and the electrician identified some things that needed to be addressed, so that was another cost.

Finally, we had to furnish the bed and breakfast guest suite which consisted of a private bath, bedroom, and living/dining room. I outfitted it with a coffee maker, bar fridge, books, a TV, internet access, Netflix, and a fireplace. The bed and breakfast was ready for a soft launch within about six months. We had racked up a significant amount of debt with all the renovations and were on our way to catching up when we realized the windows were rotting. The home inspector had indicated that they might need a fresh coat of paint, but you could actually poke your finger through some of them. Obviously, this was yet another huge and unexpected expense.

Then we began the lengthy process of marital separation. The financial stress of all of this was of course compounded with the emotional stress.

Life Lesson
Experiences have more value than money

I had found my country paradise and while it looked like a dream from the outside, on the inside it was physically and metaphorically falling apart. You never know what's really going on until you look a little closer. I re-evaluated many things during this huge life transition. One of those things was the value of money. I realized that I hated having 'stuff' around the house. For example, candles that weren't used or decorative items that had no functionality. If it didn't serve a practical purpose on a daily basis, it was just 'stuff'. And while I enjoyed doing renovations, it was a distraction and a money pit. What I realized, having daughters, is that I value experiences. I enjoy camping, amusement parks, live music, trips, and quality time with friends and family. I would much rather sacrifice stuff for experiences. Not everyone is going to agree with me and that's okay. My caution here is that money, and material things, don't buy happiness.

Photo Credit: Scott Webb from Pexels

Now we also had to divide our resources and somehow buy two separate houses. We were lucky, yet again. We found buyers who wanted to continue the bed and breakfast which made me feel better about all the work we put in and that it wouldn't go to waste. The people who bought the house have since taken the bed and breakfast to the next level. We were able to break even on the investment from the renovations, which meant that we kept the equity from the second house. Like I said, lucky.

But we were still going through a marital separation. I was working at two colleges teaching five classes, doing freelance work, and running a bed and breakfast. I was burned out and couldn't get a mortgage for myself because all my work was contract. So, I rented a townhouse temporarily and started looking for a 'real' job.

> Life Lesson
>
> ## Sometimes your expectations need a reality check
>
> *I had a roommate while I lived in North York. My vision was to be in the city and making it on my own, but I couldn't afford decent housing on what I was making alone. It was an issue of safety. With a roommate, however, I could afford somewhere that was safe and so my vision shifted. But I was still on track, I was still working toward something. And having a roommate didn't change that fact.*
>
>
>
> Photo Credit: Pexels from Pixabay

I was certainly concerned about wasting my equity by paying rent. I wanted it to be as short a time as possible. I managed to get a job and bought my own townhouse within a year. It was freeing to be financially independent. It also came with a great deal of responsibility on one income.

My overall philosophy with money through all of this has been that if you work hard, the money will come. It might seem simple, but it's worked for me. That doesn't mean that I'm oblivious to what I'm spending; I have a budget and I know what's coming in and what's going out. I've done what I had to in the short-term for financial stability and I've taken the opportunities that have come my way. I've always somehow been able to make it work. But I've always had a safety blanket with my parents and that makes a big difference.

Chapter 5
Grant me the serenity to accept the things I cannot change

I purposely left out the word 'God' in that statement. It's not that I don't believe in a higher power of some sort. It's just that I have issues with calling 'it' something specific. I have issues with the sorts of institutions that commit crimes in the name of religion. I don't know what 'it' is and so I don't want to name 'it'. I'm comfortable with that unknown. Do I think there are valuable lessons about life in the Bible (or any other religious document for that matter)? Yes, but there are also many things inside those pages that, taken literally, are quite dangerous. What I like about this prayer (because that's sort of what it is), is that it focuses on you as a person and the qualities needed to achieve balance and happiness: "Grant me the serenity to accept the things I cannot change, the courage to change the things I can, and the wisdom to know the difference" (Reinhold Niebuhr).

Photo Credit: Wokandapix from Pixabay

It was my mom who taught me this saying because she found it helpful as well. I think it was introduced to her by someone at work. I like to think that I have the courage and wisdom, but am still working on the serenity part. I'm very much like my mom and I feel we've always had a special relationship. Because our personalities are similar, we typically struggle with the same things. However, she has patience in spades and I most certainly do not. My mom would come to visit me at university on her own sometimes and I would show her around campus, my classrooms, the lecture halls, the library. We would watch movies after a day of walking around and looking at books. She would bring her pajamas and we would have a sleepover. I could easily live with my mom again. When she was living in my basement, I would put the girls to bed and then go downstairs with the baby monitor some nights. We would have a glass of wine or a cocktail and watch one of our TV shows or a movie. There was never uncomfortable silence. I could tell her the truth and not feel judged. I can't imagine having a mom that I didn't get along with, but even more than that, she's one of my best friends.

One of my favourite times with my mom is when we took my daughters to Ireland. Their dad[9] had a conference in Dublin and I desperately wanted to go along. I gave my mom two options (knowing that she loves travelling too): either watch the girls while I'm gone or come with me and we bring the girls. I didn't feel comfortable leaving the girls with anyone else for a whole week. They were only 2.5 years old and hadn't stayed over night with anyone but family. So, we packed our bags, booked our flights, and found a two-bedroom apartment to rent. This way, we would be able to have some meals at 'home'. We pushed the girls around in a double umbrella stroller all over the cobblestone streets of Dublin, to the Guinness Storehouse,

---

[9] I call my ex-husband 'the girls' dad' throughout. It's a habit I started when we separated. Ex-husband is so negative, and I don't use that term in front of the girls so why would I use it anywhere else. It's also a reminder of the beautiful gift that we share with each other.

to the zoo, to an old jail, and ate at pubs and coffee shops. It was exhausting, but it was also a blast.

The best night of the whole trip was when the girls' dad was finished his conference. He stayed with the girls at the apartment for the night while my mom and I went on a literary pub crawl. We visited all the old haunts of famous Irish authors like James Joyce, Samuel Beckett, Oscar Wilde, W.B. Yeats, and George Bernard Shaw. We drank Guinness or Bailey's and were feeling rather good by the end of the night. The people guiding the tour did performances and told stories. They gave us tasks (other than drinking) in every pub we entered. We had to find certain things and it all culminated in a round of trivia at the end of the night. Canada represented that night because my mom and I won the t-shirt, literally. After our impressive win, we both wanted to go and get a tattoo of a four-leaf clover to commemorate our trip. Funny thing though…in Dublin the tattoo parlours aren't open late at night. When we asked our tour guides to point us in the right direction, they looked at us like we were crazy. It seems like sort of a missed opportunity, but whatever. We never did get our tattoos, but the memories will stay with us forever.

A big part of my 'spiritual' development came from Girl Guides. I was involved in Girl Guides all the way through from the time I was six to about 18-years-old. I started in Brownies and my mom was one of the leaders. We learned mostly life skills and character traits. When we went camping, it was in cabins. We did hikes and bonfires and learned about safety and first aid. From ages nine to 12 years old was Girl Guides and we started camping in tents and learning more advanced outdoor skills. We would also have sleepovers and movie nights which helped us bond a great deal as a group. Then from ages 12 to 15 was Pathfinders, which again was similar, but more advanced. Girl Guides wasn't exactly the coolest activity so the longer you stayed involved, the fewer girls remained. Those that were still around though, had been involved from a young age, so we were close friends. I even became a Girl Guide leader for the newest segment of guiding called Sparks, which started at age five and prepared girls before going into Brownies. It was more story time and crafts and things, but a great steppingstone. Guiding combined two of my favourite things: learning and the outdoors.

Life Lesson
Find a place that brings you peace

I didn't realize it at the time, but nature became my church. I remember the line from the movie "Anne of Green Gables" (with Meghan Follows) where she describes praying out in an empty field looking up to the sky and just feeling a prayer. Why do you have to pray in a church, why does it have to involve a reverend, priest, or minister? Shouldn't you have a direct relationship with God? Living in the country though, there was plenty of nature and whenever I was upset or angry, I would walk up the dead-end road and sit on this huge white rock in between the farm fields. When I sat there, I could see all around and everything looked so tiny. I can remember hearing the birds and the crickets and feeling closer to nature. It made me feel calm and gave me perspective and it was a safe place for me to vent and stew without harming anyone else. From then on, I needed a place like this in my life.

Photo Credit: PhotoMIX Ltd. From Pexels

One camping trip was to Camp Samac. The Brownies were staying in cabins (usually you didn't tent until Guides) and when it was time for lights out, the girls in my cabin kept talking. My mom came in to warn them that if they couldn't keep it down, she would put them out on the front porch. That way they wouldn't be keeping anyone else awake. My mom also knew that the mosquitoes would be horrific. I promptly rolled over and went to sleep. The rest of the girls thought my mom was bluffing and continued their chatter even though I warned them that she meant business. Sure enough, 10 minutes later, three girls were sitting on the cabin porch in their pajamas getting eaten alive by mosquitoes. I was comfy in my sleeping bag.

My values came from many members in my family, but my mom was always extremely patient and extremely fair. I suppose some of my values did come from going to church when I was young. We went to nursery school and for quite some time I did try to read the Bible. I always got to the part where they list all the names and who's related to who and that was enough. I knew the main stories though and the values they taught, but from an early age had questions that no one could answer, or they chose not to answer. I used to watch my mom getting ready for church. She had a vanity table in her bedroom and I would watch her do her hair and makeup. There's something very calming about people watching, and I don't mean the kind you do at the mall (though that's entertaining as well). Watching someone perform habitual activities is mesmerizing. I vividly remember the smell of her lipstick and the suede coat with the fur collar she would wear for special outings. The combined smell of these things will be forever imprinted in my soul. When my mom went back to work, we stopped going to church; the weekends just weren't long enough to get all the domestic things done and fit in a 30-minute drive to church and back. I wasn't upset in the least, though I know that my mom was disappointed.

Camping was another value inspiring experience. The smell of pine needles in the forest, crashing waves at the beach, the feel of sand between your toes, and crackling campfires at night. We would go camping to provincial parks on weekends or on family vacations in the summer: all of these in a pickup truck and RV. We went to Disney World when I was three and 11, the east coast when I was five and 13, the west coast when I was eight, and many other places in between. Usually, my grandma would come with us. My grandpa didn't like to be away from home, so coming with us was her way to scratch her itch to travel. And it meant that I have many great memories with my grandma. Curled up with her on the pull-out sofa, walking on the beach with her early in the morning while everyone else slept in, and eating ice cream every place we could find. My grandma loved ice cream.

Even though my first trip on a plane wasn't until my early twenties, I did quite a bit of travelling in North America with my family. It was interesting to experience different places, see the history, and enjoy the vastly different landscapes that Canada and the USA had to offer. Even though it wasn't that different culturally, it gave me an appreciation and comfort level with travelling that I greatly appreciated. I've been to many other places since then. Sometimes I was travelling for work, like: San Francisco, California; New Orleans, Louisiana; and sometimes for fun like resorts in Panama and Jamaica, or cities like Prague, Czech Republic; Paris, France; Krakow and Warsaw, Poland; Berlin, Germany; and Dublin, Ireland. I think travelling gives me that same feeling as when I sat out on my white rock in the middle of a farm field. It puts things in perspective and lets you know how small you really are in the world. On the flip side though, it lets you know that people are people and that you can't really make assumptions about anyone. Everyone has a story.

When I couldn't be with nature, and to avoid conflict with my dad, I hid in my bedroom listening to music. It wasn't just listening; it was taking solace. Sometimes it was top 40 or cheerful oldies, sometimes angry metal, sometimes rap or reggae (which really got my dad going), and sometimes teen angst alternative.

This was back in the day of cassette tapes and trying to catch your favourite song on the radio so you could record a crappy version of it with the DJ talking and a horrible screech transitioning to the next song. Or when the tape got caught and wrinkled and you had to use your finger or a pencil to wind it back up again, but it never quite sounded the same afterwards. The introduction of CDs in my teens was monumental!

And then there were the mail order program, through which you could get like 20 CDs for $1, but not really. I don't remember the ins and outs, but my sister and I somehow found a loophole that if we ordered a bunch and then returned a certain amount, we could keep the rest for free…or something to that effect. And then we learned (from our jobs at the gas station/post office) that you didn't have to pay for postage if you kept the box and wrote 'return to sender' on the outside. It was brilliant! We managed to transition almost our whole tape collection to CD for about $10 each, I think. And then, you didn't have to fast forward through a song, you could just skip! True, you had to worry about scratching the disc, but it was so much easier than wrinkled cassette tapes.

My grandparents loved music too. They always had a radio playing unless they were watching TV. It played throughout the main floor. Every Friday night they would go out for dinner and dancing to a little place called The Hole in the Wall.

Life Lesson
Music connects with your soul

Even if you're not a musician, music has a unique way of touching your soul. It has a way of bringing emotions to the surface so you can experience them and let them go. It has a way of soothing or healing your hurts, letting you know that you're understood, and helping you jump hurdles and turn corners. It can literally start your day off a little better. I remember having a clock radio when I was a teenager, and I set the alarm to a radio station. It was a nice, soft way to greet the morning and sometimes it put a little more pep in my step. I missed that experience until I got a cell phone that connects to my music playlists. Now I have that same experience and I share it with my girls too. We may even have a little dance party in the morning before we get going. Music is a powerful thing.

Photo Credit: StockSnap from Pixabay

There were plenty of times that my parents went on trips without us and during those times we stayed with Grams and Gramps. They would even take us with them on their Friday date night. I remember Gramps going up to have a bath, shave, and comb his hair. He would put on his nice clothes and wear his suspenders. When he came downstairs, he would smell like cologne. Their favourite dinner was Chinese food. It was something that we didn't really get at home because my dad was more of a meat and potatoes man.

Then my sister and I would go to sleep in the bedroom upstairs, the one that my mom and aunt used to share. We would fall asleep in the double bed that curved down a little at the edges, so you almost felt like you were going to fall out. We would sleep in the sheets that smelled like grandma, a mix of perfume and hand cream. Then we would hear the clock on the mantel chime and Gramps' hoarse cough before we dropped off to sleep. We always had a great time. When we woke up in the morning, we would have cereal with chocolate chips for breakfast, or cold pie, pizza, or breaded chicken.

My grandparents built their house after they married, buying supplies with each paycheque. That house had so many memories. At one point there were four generations living on approximately one acre. My grandparents and their children in the main house (which was only a two bedroom), my great grandparents in the little house next door (which was probably only 500 square feet and didn't have running water), and my great, great grandparents lived in what would eventually be the workshop. There was an old-fashioned water pump by the driveway which was still functioning long into my childhood. The house, property, and outbuildings were my grandparents' up until my grandfather passed away in 2018. Now, there will be a townhouse development built on the property, one acre in the middle of suburbia. My family watched that area grow from a dirt road and farm fields into current day Courtice, Ontario.

My grandmother had a heart attack in 2007 and it changed the rest of her life. She couldn't live life at the same pace. She was active and social despite her age. But after the heart attack she had to slow down and couldn't do the things she loved. She had a second heart attack a year later and this time it killed her. I had just been married and was starting my sales position. I had my grandparents over for Christmas dinner that year and I was so thankful to have that memory. We got the call in the middle of the night and went to the hospital first thing in the morning. I saw her, but it wasn't really Grams. I kissed her cheek and tried to say goodbye, but how do you really do that? I'm told that she hung on until the minister got there to pray for her soul.

After she died, we all received a laminated letter from Grandma. The letter essentially said that she decided against taking medication for her heart condition because she didn't want to prolong the inevitable. Nor could she continue living half a life. That last year when her body was failing, I think it was slowly killing her soul as well. She had no joy for life. Her letter said that she wasn't afraid, that God was waiting for her and for us to have faith. I was really angry at first. How could she make that decision for all of us? Wasn't that selfish, to purposely accelerate the next heart attack and make it more severe by not taking her medication?

It took me a while to understand that if she had taken her medication and stayed alive for a prolonged period, that wouldn't have been her either. Just like seeing her in that hospital bed.

Life Lesson
Death is just the next chapter

Death is a hard thing because it's the unknown yet again. You don't know where your loved ones are or whether you will see them again. You don't know when it will happen or how. Sometimes it's sudden and other times it drags on. My grandma loved cardinals. I know that cardinals are a symbol for loved ones coming to visit us, but they have an extra special meaning for me because my Grams' house was filled with them. She had sun catchers, wooden ornaments, and decorative plates, all of cardinals. Whenever I see one, I feel grateful. At Grams' funeral, I remember everyone talking about what a good person she was, how she volunteered in her community, she was kind, an upstanding citizen, and all that. All those things were true, but it didn't hit the mark for me. The Grams I knew was a little bit mischievous. She liked to have her cake and eat it too. She was fun. Maybe that was the kid in me bringing out the kid in her. When I picture Grams up in heaven, I think she's probably eating ice cream and watching Pretty Woman or Crocodile Dundee.

Photo Credit: Krisztina Papp from Pexels

It sounds horrible, but we all thought my Gramps wouldn't last long after losing Grams. Grams was his life. He lived another 10 years, which is amazing. He learned to do so many things on his own that he never had before, everyday things that my Grams would always do for him. He learned to make a grocery list and go shopping. He learned to do his finances and manage bills. He learned to prepare food. He had help of course, but it was quite impressive.

When he passed, he had several health issues, but ultimately his heart failed. I think he stuck around to see his great-grandchildren grow a bit so he could tell her about it when he got to heaven. Somehow, I can picture my Grams scolding him and saying, "What took you so long?"

Life Lesson
Pets are family members too

Maggie was always on high alert and loved playing fetch; Hunter was mostly laid back and he was a nose dog, trotting through the brush with his nose to the ground, picking up various scents. The dogs were so good with Cami and Maya, even before they were born. I have so many photos of Hunter resting his head on my pregnant belly. He was fiercely protective of the girls; when I would take the babies on the dog walk, he would get between the girls and anyone coming our way. I learned a great deal from having dogs. They are givers, not takers. They are always there, but really, they don't ask for much. I found a snuggle from a dog could recharge my batteries or help me unwind after a busy day. Having dogs also forced me to get outside and go for walks. Witnessing their pure joy chasing each other around or walking trails through the forest was soul food.

Photo Credit: Marcia Allyn Luke

Photo Credit: Marcia Allyn Luke

More recently, I've lost two pets in my life. When my daughters were born, we had two Hungarian Vizslas that were three years old. One was Maggie and we had her from the time she was a puppy. The other one was Hunter, who we adopted at the age of one. Hunter and Maggie behaved very much like brother and sister. The night we brought Hunter home, he and Maggie played in the backyard until one in the morning.

When we woke up, Maggie looked at us and the words on her face were clear: "Well that was fun, but what's he still doing here?" She liked having him around, but was a bit sulky. Hunter had no such qualms. He was extremely affectionate and would take all the attention he could get. Maggie learned after a couple of months that if she didn't quit sulking and come out of her hiding place, she wasn't going to get any love. They got along splendidly after that.

One morning, Hunter didn't wake up. I was about to head to work, my first day at a new job. The girls' dad called me upstairs and I could hear in his voice that something was terribly wrong. Hunter was still laying on his dog bed in the crate he shared with Maggie. He wasn't moving. He was still warm, but his nose was dry. We were beside ourselves. We carried him downstairs in his dog bed and put him in the car. I was begging him the whole time to hang on. Then I gave him what would be the last kiss and the girls' dad drove to the vet with hopes of saving him. I got the girls into my vehicle and drove them to school on my way to my new job, waiting for the phone call that eventually came: he was gone.

There were no signs of anything wrong, but the vet speculated that there was maybe a heart defect that went undetected. It was too quick. I cried all the way to work and then pulled myself together. Work was a good distraction.

Maggie was strong and healthy, until she was eight and a half years old. She developed a lump on her ear which the vet recommended removing, so we did. It came back with a vengeance within six months and this time the vet took a biopsy and told us it was cancerous. They took her whole ear flap this time and it was a difficult surgery for her. She wasn't herself for about a month and I was afraid it was over. But then our bouncy Maggie was back and better than ever. She had an excellent summer, but eventually the cancer came back, this time in her blood stream. It was only a matter of time.

It was a tough call to make, but when Maggie stopped enjoying her walks, when she needed to be carried up and down stairs and into the back of my vehicle, and when her eating habits became irregular, I knew it was almost time. Then she started throwing up randomly. A lump developed on her neck that grew extremely quickly. At nine and a half years old, her joie de vivre had disappeared almost completely. I scheduled the appointment and took her in. She always hated the vet, but she came in with me quite willingly. She immediately laid down on the dog bed provided which was unusual. She was calm through the whole process. I was a wreck. I happened to have my hand on her chest as she left this world and I was glad I did. I would have missed her passing otherwise. I stayed with her afterwards and held her and kissed her. I didn't think I could leave, but I also didn't want my last memory of her to be of her cold, empty body. So, I stayed until I felt I couldn't anymore, and then I left her there. It was one of the hardest things I've ever had to do. I think (and hope) somehow she knew and was grateful. My dogs were a part of the family. They will always be in my heart and I am forever changed as a person because of the gift of their presence. I hope they know how much they were (and still are) loved.

I've often questioned the meaning of life. I still do in fact. I don't call myself religious, but I would say that I am spiritual. I don't believe in a god or gods, but I believe in some kind of metaphysical force. I believe in past and future lives. I believe in karma. I believe in spirits and synchronicity. I also believe in willpower, determination, choice, and individuality. But I think all these things come together to form this crazy thing called life. So, what is the purpose of life? I believe that a big part of it is to be with friends and family, to have experiences big and small, to let go of judgment, to be grateful for what we have in life, and to act with kindness. Is that all though? If there's a heaven, is there a hell? What will I teach my girls?

- To be fearless, or rather to act in spite of fear for that which you believe.
- To enjoy the moments, especially the small ones, because if you buy into the hype, the big ones often disappoint.
- To put less pressure on the 'big' moments, enjoy them for what they are.
- That happiness means not reacting to others, but looking inside yourself.
- To be yourself and that being untrue to yourself can only result in unhappiness.
- We are connected to all things; we need water, air, earth, and fire. Respect nature. Enjoy it, but leave it the way you found it.

And I'm still working on the rest. I'm hoping my girls teach me a few things along the way too.

Chapter 6
Take care of your body; it's the only one you get

I realize looking back, that some of the most difficult times in my life have been my least physically active. I ended up feeling angry, sad, depressed, anxious, though at the time, I didn't make the connection. And while I've had a love/hate relationship with exercise most of my life, I know that I need it to be happy as well as healthy.

At different times in my life, I've been drawn to different activities and that's okay. Just keep moving. Keep trying different things, until you find what works for you at that time. If your body isn't happy, your mind and your spirit won't be happy either.

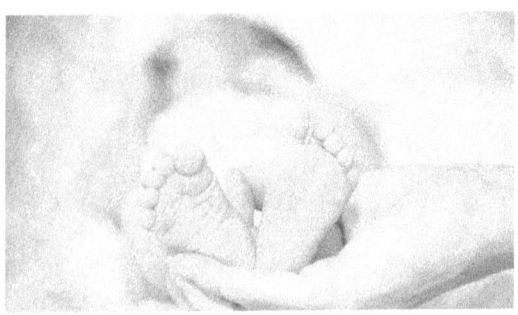

Photo Credit: Rene Asmussen from Pexels

I will preface this chapter by disclosing that I am clumsy. It's at least partially genetic, but the combination of my pace and my general discoordination don't help either. There are very few physical activities that I can do well without practicing a bunch. Running was one of the few. I've been a runner off and on throughout my life. In elementary school, I ran track. I was small and fast, and I enjoyed the competition, in part because my sister would challenge me to races. Given her extra three and a half years and the fact that she's now five foot 10 inches tall, she had a significant advantage. She always won and that made me mad, but it made me want to do better. In many ways, she fostered my competitive spirit. I ran track (all distances) and did high jump. It was exhilarating to be good at something.

In grade six, I started gymnastics and band. Gymnastics I started because my best friend was doing it, and band I started because my sister was doing it. Both were challenging and fun. Gymnastics was one of the first times that I felt true pressure to perform. I was good, but I certainly wasn't one of the best and we had to perform to a certain level as a team.

Life Lesson
Watch where you're going

I was walking across the playground one day and happened to walk in front of the swing set. I was a little too close and a girl swung out at just the right (or wrong) moment and kicked me in the head. I remember my sister running over to see if I was okay. That was probably my first concussion. I remember laying on the couch in the 'nice' living room (the one reserved for company) with my mom in the kitchen getting dinner ready. She would wake me up every half hour or so and did this all night. I didn't really understand at the time, but I recovered quickly. I did learn to watch where I was going, though it took a little longer to sink in.

Photo Credit: Robin McPherson from Pexels

The best gymnasts were also part of a private club and the message was loud and clear: if you weren't part of a private club, you wouldn't make it on the high school team. I found out later this wasn't the case and that I could have joined. But these things work out for a reason, or in this case, don't work out.

Band was good for me. Though it's not a physical activity it certainly kept me balanced as a creative outlet. I started with the recorder as many do, and then tried the clarinet, saxophone, and, finally, the flute. Basically, everything that my sister brought home. Both her and I took to the flute. Once again, it was something that I picked up easily, but I loved it, so I put in the time to practice and improve. It was rewarding to be the one helping other people learn a piece of music. And it spoke to my heart in a big way. There are still pieces of music that are etched in my memory because of how they made me feel when I played them. The school board was trying something new for their enrichment programs: Honour Band. It would be made up of the best students from the whole school board and at the end of the year, we would play at the Academy Theatre in Lindsay, Ontario. It was a big deal and I remember being nervous, but I tried out anyways. I made it and I loved it! Honour Band challenged me and pushed me to the next level. It was humbling and motivating. People even had to pay for their tickets to attend the final performance. It was thrilling.

In high school, I ran cross country. After running track for so many years, it was the logical choice. I tried out for volleyball and rugby, but quickly realized that individual sports were more my speed (pun intended). Likely because I didn't have much experience playing team sports. Unless you count softball when I was 10, which I don't. Let me explain. The softball team that I was on was pretty sad. The coach, who was doing this out of the kindness of his heart, didn't really teach me anything. I remember his face going red frequently and a great deal of yelling. It was a confusing and somewhat scarring experience. And it certainly didn't teach me about team sports.

Cross country was great in some ways because it pushed me to do more, but at the same time longer distances are what made me start to hate running. Some days you would have a great run and some days would suck. There was also this crazy expectation that you would train. Running was something I had always been good at. I didn't have to train. But now, I needed to condition myself which meant running at home for certain distances (which I rarely ever did to the full extent), interval training, and hills. Hills were my nemesis; I always struggled with them. My sister would barrel up a hill in no time and she would be tired, but exhilarated. It just drained me.

My cross-country coach was great: passionate, easy going, approachable, and dedicated. And he was a genuinely nice guy. He did not understand how to coach girls though. Or maybe it was just me. Once again, I found myself the weakest link on the team and even though it was once again an individual sport, the performance of all members counted. My coach would approach me before a race and say things like "I'm counting on you" or "it's all up to you." This may have worked well with the boys (or other girls for that matter), bringing out their competitive spirit. But after he spoke with me and turned to leave, I would start hyperventilating or, to my dismay, crying. Not the best way to start a race where you need to breathe and pace yourself. Putting pressure on me was not helpful at all—if he had said "just do your best and have fun" I would have been in a much better position. He was certainly an improvement from my softball coach though; there was no yelling.

Life Lesson
If I only had a brain…or a new one

My second concussion happened because of gymnastics. We would practice in the school yard where one person would bend over and act as the vault and the other would jump over top. The first time I was the vault, I didn't expect the amount of force that came down on me and I fell forward headfirst. I remember seeing stars that time. I also used to practice in the living room and can't count the number of times I tried to do a back walkover and landed on my head. I would get up and shake it off, but often I would be nauseated afterwards. This is maybe why I'm not upset that I discontinued gymnastics after elementary school. It probably wasn't the best activity for my brain and there wasn't as much awareness about concussions then.

Photo Credit: Inkdrop

Of course, I do wish I had trained a little more consistently, but that wouldn't necessarily have changed my weakest link position. I'm sure it would have improved my performance though and that's what I didn't understand at the time. I was used to running for the joy of it and being on a team made it feel like work.

In university I was introduced to the gym. I started doing some weights and loved the muscle burn and feeling strong. I stuck with that for several years. At the same time, I was rock climbing. I once went to a climbing gym in Markham on a field trip in high school and loved it so much that when the universities and colleges came around to do their presentations that was on my list of preferences. I chose my university partly because they had a climbing gym on site. They had turned an old squash court (eventually two) into a climbing wall. I started climbing with one of the guys that lived in my residence and we continued to climb together all the way through university, even afterwards, and occasionally even today. It was something that I found I progressed at quickly and I was relatively flexible which also helped me. I even ended up working at a rock-climbing gym in Guelph after graduating from university, teaching newcomers how to belay, and helping with kids' birthday parties.

Parenting Perspective
If you're not sure, just go to the hospital

To catch the bus in the morning, my sister and I (and a few other kids that lived on our dead-end road) had to walk down to the stop sign. It was winter and it was snowing, and the plough hadn't cleared our road yet, so my sister and I were walking in the grooves left by the tires. She yelled "car" and I immediately started toward the side of the road that I thought was closest. Did I mention it was snowing? So that meant visibility was poor for both me and for cars. Unfortunately, I was closer to the left side and started heading right and was hit by a Chevette. It caught me in the right hip and sent me airborne over the top of the car which skidded into the ditch. Once again, my sister ran over to see if I was okay. My biggest concern was an oral French exam that I had that day. Everything seemed to be in working order, so when I heard the bus coming, we all ran to get to school.

My mom called me at school during first period class—my neighbour, who had hit me, had walked to my house to tell my mom and they called the police. When everyone arrived, they started looking in snowbanks for me since they couldn't find anyone around. Over the phone, my mom asked me if I

> wanted to press charges and since it was my neighbour and technically my mistake, I said no.
>
>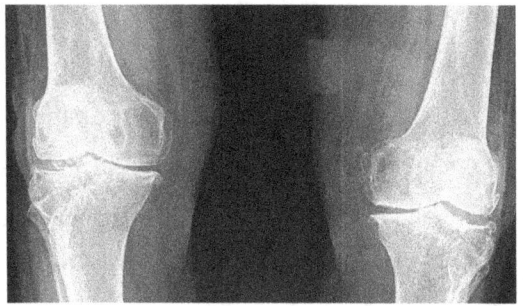
>
> Photo Credit: Taokinesis from Pixabay
>
> After school, my mom and dad asked me if I wanted to go to the hospital, but clearly nothing was broken and there wasn't even a bruise. As a result, now my right leg is shorter than the other and I will probably end up with arthritis in my hip. I may have still developed arthritis even if I had treatment, but it probably would have been a good idea to see a doctor. Though this is a Parenting Perspective, it's really a life lesson too. If you get into a physical altercation with a Chevette, just go to the hospital.

When I was home in the summers, my sister and I would go to the gym, play squash, run, or bike together. She was always a good influence on my physical activity. We tried a few classes: cross fit, Pilates, yoga, boxercise. Whatever we were doing, we did it together.

Like many university and college students, I was victim to the 'frosh five'. But the additional weight hit me every year, so by the time I graduated it was a 'graduate 20'. I worked extremely hard when I was in North York running and working out, eating a balanced diet, and staying away from bad treats. I lost almost all the weight I put on when I was in university. I started out running five kilometres. Then I started running five kilometres to the gym, working out, then running home. Then I started running seven kilometres straight. Once I got past the first five, it felt almost like I could run forever. My sister and I started doing races together, not necessarily to win (the people that win these races are usually training for the Boston Marathon or something). We simply aimed to finish longer distances each time. We did five, then 10, then I started training for a half marathon. Why not? The summer I started working in publishing, I was training for a half marathon (21-kilometres), had five weddings to attend, and was a bridesmaid in three of them. I finished the half marathon in two hours and 17 minutes. It was a huge accomplishment. I would like to do a full marathon at some point just to say I did it, but time is ticking.

Then I got married, and we both put on a few extra pounds. The happy pounds. What finally got me out of that rut was an author I worked with. I described my love/hate relationship with running and she recommended a book. It was called *Born to Run* by Christopher McDougall and it was a great read. It started a few things for me. I became vegetarian (and then vegan) and I started barefoot running. The idea behind barefoot running was that 'primitive' civilizations would run all day long and they didn't have Nike shoes to help them. They ran by landing on the ball of their foot first, in a soft, gradual roll from the outside to the inside and barely even touching the heel. The message in the book is that this is the way we were born to run. I tried it and it felt much more natural. Barefoot running was a little harder on my calves to start, but otherwise was excellent.

In *Born to Run*, the transition to being vegan was also inspired by the examination of 'primitive' civilizations largely untouched by modern or Western society. They ate mostly plant-based diets and only ate meat once a month or so when they could hunt something big enough to eat. Guess how long it takes to chase down an animal before it overheats and lies down? Approximately 42 kilometres, or the distance of the modern-day marathon!

Many health issues were examined and blamed on factory farming, overconsumption of meat, use of hormones and chemicals, etc.[10] Why would I continue to put all this bad food in my body? Especially when my family had a history of heart disease? If I could go vegan, why wouldn't I? So, I read some more books, including Alicia Silverstone's *The Kind Diet*[11] and learned how to be a healthy, nutritionally balanced vegan. I made some of the best food I've ever made in my life. I learned how to use spices effectively, I tried vegetables I'd never heard of, and I was completely satisfied with one exception. Milk alternatives are excellent—cheese alternatives suck. Or they did when I was vegan anyways. As a bonus, I began to lose weight, ending up at the same weight I was in high school. I felt lighter and had more energy than I had in a long time. I also felt better running that I ever had.

I mentioned earlier that I had difficulty getting pregnant. That's not quite true. I had difficulty staying pregnant. I got pregnant easily but would miscarry at about the five-

---

[10] McDougall, C. (2011). *Born to Run: A Hidden Tribe, Superathletes, and the Greatest Race the World* (Reprint ed.). New York, NY: Vintage.

[11] Silverstone, A. (2011). *The Kind Diet: A Simple Guide to Feeling Great, Losing Weight, and Saving the Planet* (Illustrated ed.). Emmaus, PA: Rodale Books.

or six-week mark. I went to get it checked out and found out that I have something called a balanced chromosomal translocation. I'm no geneticist, but here's my understanding: when I was conceived, two of my chromosomes switched content, but a balanced or roughly equal amount of content. So, this condition doesn't display as any abnormality for me, but since my eggs only take half of my genetic material, sometimes it's the right half and sometimes it's the wrong half. Which meant that my miscarriages were a result of genetically faulty eggs. My body would recognize the problem and discard the fetus, sooner rather than later, for which I was grateful. I've only met one other person with this condition; she lost her babies much later in the process and my heart broke for her. It's a difficult thing to experience, in any capacity.[12]

The doctor described it much like a lottery; you never know when you're going to get lucky. I kept trying, hoping every month that it would literally be a 'good egg'. After three years of this and miscarrying many times, I was ready to skip right to adoption. I was afraid of going

---

[12] Lynn, D., Luke, M. A., Philip, J., Corbin, S., Wooten, S., Speicher, S., Peters, K., ... Tremblay, L. (2019). *Silent Grief, Healing and Hope: 15 Inspirational Stories of Infertility, Miscarriage, and Child Loss*. Your Shift Matters.

through the in vitro fertilization (IVF) process and still ending up with nothing.

But the girls' dad really wanted to try fertility treatment just once to see if we could have our own kids. I agreed, partly because I just wanted to try something different and partly because I realized that this was my first test as a parent. I was going to let my fear stop me from even trying and that's certainly not what I would teach my 'hypothetical' children.

The doctor would take as many eggs as possible, fertilize them all, incubate them for five to six days, and then take a biopsy. The biopsy, and subsequent genetic screening, would tell them which embryos were genetically viable and they would only implant the best ones.

I had two genetically viable embryos of the 17. Two made it through the incubation and biopsy and were shown to be genetically viable. Both embryos were implanted on Christmas Eve of 2013, I was 34 years old. At the time they were called baby A and baby B, but they would become Maya and Cami.

Parenting Perspective
Children are parasites

I ended up having in vitro fertilization which took on the first try (lucky!) and resulted in fraternal twin girls. And then I had a twin pregnancy. I was incredibly sick throughout the entire pregnancy. It started with heartburn and then at six weeks the morning sickness kicked in, except that it was more like all day. I couldn't keep anything down. I remember going to my ultrasound (after vomiting for three days straight), begging for some relief. I took a mixing bowl with me in case I had to throw up in the car. They gave me an antinausea prescription and I was so relieved. And then I couldn't keep that down either. I had to go to the hospital and get an IV laced with Gravol to get my stomach settled enough that I could take the prescription.

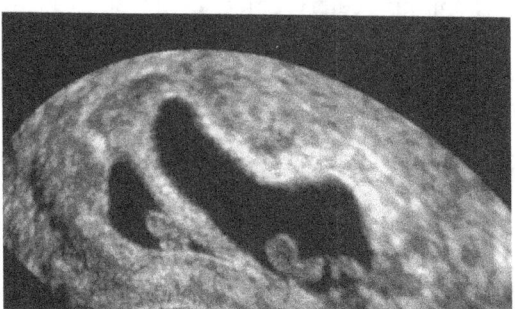

Photo Credit: Marcia Allyn Luke

I was still vegan at the start of my pregnancy and researching how to make sure the babies got what they needed. Though the prescription helped with the nausea, it certainly didn't alleviate it completely and some things still made me sick. The bigger problem was the heartburn—I couldn't eat onion, garlic, soy, spice of any kind, too many vegetables…I was basically eating off the kids' menu. And then the cravings started. I craved meat and dairy. I dreamed about tuna melts and cheeseburgers. And about two months into the pregnancy, I finally caved. There were so few things I could eat to begin with, and I was feeling so miserable. I gave the babies what they wanted.

I still tried to keep many of the good habits I had learned, starting each day with a protein shake, and munching on carrots, hummus, celery, fruit, etc. I enjoyed meat so much as a result of my babies that, to my dismay, I still haven't gone back to being vegan. From then on, with the help of prescription medication for both acid reflux and nausea, combined with and a toddler diet (with no flavour, sauce, or spice of any kind), I managed well enough. I affectionately called the girls 'parasites' since they were literally sucking the life out of me. But I realize now that it's not just during pregnancy. They take and take and occasionally give back, but it's the joy you find in the giving that keeps you going.

Even though I've never really considered myself to be overweight, I've struggled to maintain the balance required for a healthy lifestyle. I have a sweet tooth and a salty one. After having the girls, I lost the weight quickly and kept it off for quite some time. I was still very emotional about six weeks into parenthood and then the girls developed acid reflux. Every feeding became a nightmare. They would get hungry and cry at the same time, but I had to feed each one of them carefully and slowly, so they didn't vomit it all up. Then I had to burp them extensively to ensure the same. All the while, the other twin is screaming bloody murder and I'm crying, and I don't know how to feed them both at the same time. My mom walked in one day and I was crying, a whole box of Kleenex used and crumpled on the coffee table.

My mom told me she thought it was time to go to the doctor. And I went on medication for postpartum. It helped immensely, though it took some time to get the dosage right.

Life Lesson
Ask for help

Despite the medication for postpartum depression, I was still struggling after about four and a half months. I felt like I had a dark monster living inside me. I knew that I wasn't myself, but I couldn't do anything about it. I reacted with tears over simple things, but more often than not I reacted with anger. I had a difficult time engaging with the girls. Staying distanced and checking out was one of my survival mechanisms, but it also meant that I wasn't always there for them. I was trying to avoid the negative, but not benefiting from the positive either.

My turning point came when I was sitting at the table one day, cutting up cheese for the girls to eat. They started to lose it over something so small and I had the urge to drive the knife I held into my arm. It wasn't a suicidal urge at all. It was more like "I don't want to feel this pain anymore so I will cause another kind of pain to distract myself". I didn't do anything to myself that day, but I realized I needed more help.

Photo Credit: RODNAE Productions from Pexels

A friend told me to call the public health nurse since I had never received my postnatal visit. She sent me to a support group and told me to ask my doctor to refer me to a local Women's Mental Health Program. It was nerve wracking, but at that stage I was willing to accept any help that was being offered. I completed a year long program designed for women with postpartum mood disorders (PPMD), largely based on cognitive behavioural therapy. It was extremely helpful, but more importantly, it was delivered by a social worker. Up until then, my experiences with therapy hadn't been positive: counselling, psychologists, etc. In sessions, I found we were either stuck in the talking stage and not doing anything to remedy the problem or that I was coming to the table with my own answers and extraordinarily little insight given by the 'professional'.

Life Lesson
Listen to your body

I've always had headaches. From a young age I would get migraines. I feel that everyone has a particular weakness in their body, somewhere that stress affects them most. I would get so excited when I was a kid, anticipating a field trip or vacation, that I would end up down and out with a migraine and miss it altogether. I realize now that it was anxiety, but that label wasn't really used when I was growing up. Eventually, I learned to manage it better. I didn't really try to alleviate the anxiety, but I worked with it, running through scenarios in my head to prepare myself. I became what they call 'high-functioning'. But the anxiety was still there.

Other things affect my headaches as well: weather, hormones, sometimes food, etc. I took a course in university to learn about migraines and triggers and how to manage them. If I couldn't get rid of a headache, then I did what I had to in order to get some sleep. Sometimes Advil worked, sometimes not. I started using cold cloths and then ice packs which would help reduce the inflammation enough to sleep. Today, I still read as much information as I can on headaches and anxiety since there's always new information available. I've learned to listen to my body as well. I might not be able to get rid of my weaknesses, but I can learn and listen.

Photo Credit: Avi_Acl from Pixabay

My experience with this social worker was wonderful and exactly what I needed: a balance of talking and understanding, normalizing what I was going through, and problem solving. I've had subsequent experiences with a different social worker and found it to be similar. I guess it's kind of like dating…you have to try a few out before you find a fit. What I learned is this: even if you can't ask for help yet, talk about what you're going through with someone you trust and you might find they have something helpful to offer. Just talk, that's all.

Then, another huge hurdle came my way. We were working in the backyard putting in a patio. We had been levelling the limestone and had string around and across the space, held in place by plastic 18-inch stakes. After the levelling was complete, I went around pulling out the stakes, some of which were tough to remove because the dirt and limestone had been packed well. The backyard had a walkout basement with a recessed doorway. So, coming out of the walkout basement you would cross a smaller patio and climb four steps to the main portion of the backyard, which was where we were laying a secondary patio. One of the stakes was at the edge of the recessed area and the earth around it was bordered by railway ties. Unfortunately, the stake closest to the railway ties came out of the ground quite easily. I heaved on it and it popped out of the ground and, if you can picture it, I did a Looney Tunes type spiral with my arms trying to catch myself. I was unsuccessful.

I fell backwards and down into the recessed patio and hit headfirst on the brick. I'm about five feet, five inches, but add on the four steps and it was probably about a seven-foot fall. I remember that moment seeming to last forever. The girls' dad was directly across from me and I saw the panic in his eyes. He reached out to try and grab my hands, but it was too late. My head cracked on the brick like a coconut and started bleeding. Thank goodness the girls weren't home. The ambulance came, I was vomiting and writhing on the ground. I think the experience was at least as traumatizing for the girls' dad as it was for me, maybe more. The result was three staples in my head and a black eye which my brain gave me from the inside out (that's how hard the impact was). For more than a week, I was sitting on the couch or in bed with limited activity. I could listen to music or audio books quietly, but no screen time, no bright lights. I could go for short walks or spend time outside with sunglasses and a hat. Then I gradually started to do some work from home to get back to my new normal.

Now, the headaches I had from my concussions were quite different from migraines. It's hard to describe the difference, but migraines come from the inside out and the concussion pain was more from the outside in. I saw ophthalmologists, optometrists, chiropractors, etc. some of which masqueraded as concussion experts. Since there's no official designation for a concussion expert, practically anyone can call themselves one. What I found was that the chiropractors didn't do anything differently from visits in the past. I was still experiencing symptoms like chronic headaches, sensitivity to light, difficulty concentrating, fatigue, irritability, trouble finding words or recalling information, issues with balance, difficulty sleeping, sensitivity to loud noise or multiple sources of noise, etc. My doctor had been concussed before and while I'm not glad that she had to experience it, I was incredibly grateful that she understood exactly what it was like. As a result, she took my symptoms very seriously and referred me to the Sunnybrook Traumatic Head Injury Clinic to try and get some answers.

I was impressed at how thorough the examination was at Sunnybrook. I met with several specialists who were all part of the same program for a more integrated approach. There were a couple of important things that I learned at Sunnybrook. First, your brain remembers every injury. Even if it heals, any future injuries are compounded. All the times I hit my head as a kid were having a marked effect on my recovery from what I call 'the big one'. They said that my recovery was taking longer as a result of my previous injuries. These are the possible/likely concussions I had along the way:

- The Swing Set, kicked in the head (age 8).
- A Human Vault, headfirst onto ground (age 11).
- The Back Walkover, landed on my head multiple times (age 12).
- The Chevette, hit by a car (age 14).

- Drywall Divot, ran into a wall (age 14).
- Lola's T-bone, car accident with my driver's side hit (age 31).
- Looney Tunes/The Big One, fell backwards and down onto patio (age 36).
- Staircase Tumble, fell down the stairs (age 38).
- Stella's Rear End, car accident, I was rear-ended (age 40).

Another thing I learned was that most of the recovery takes place in the first two years after a concussion and any improvement beyond that is likely to be small. Sunnybrook referred me to a neurologist after their assessment who was meant to help manage the chronic pain. The neurologist explained the recovery process like this: your brain's main way of healing is time, so we manage the pain while the healing is still happening in the background. He prescribed medication for me to help with the pain and it did help immensely. He indicated that I should try going off the medication every three months or so and see how I felt. I stayed on it for about a year.

At the time, I was teaching professional writing at a local college. The students had gotten used to the fact that I had to turn off most of the fluorescent lights in the classroom due to headaches. I had them give presentations and one of the groups chose the topic of legalizing marijuana (about six months before it became legal recreationally in Canada). Their presentation also covered Cannabidiol (CBD) oil and its uses for concussion recovery, which I had never heard before. Pure CBD oil has no Tetrahydrocannabinol (THC) which is the psychoactive property. You can get blends of both CBD and THC, but their presentation referred to CBD oil.[13] So, I ordered it online and found that I could replace the prescription medication with CBD. I was thrilled since there were no side effects to the CBD oil and I felt better off the medication. It was likely a combination of timing—I'm more than willing to admit that in the beginning, CBD probably wouldn't have been enough, and I needed that year on the meds to reach a point where I could effectively transition. This was one of my first experiences with alternative medicine.

When I went for my first appointment with the laser specialists, I described my situation in detail, going through my history carefully. The doctor there said: "you know, 80% recovered is pretty good" and I thought, oh

---

[13] Professional Writing Class. (Personal Communication, 2018).

no. This guy doesn't get it, he's going to say they can't help me. I'm going to be stuck in this limbo where I'm not quite myself forever. I won't be able to do things that I love. I won't be able to enjoy life. Work and play will always be a struggle. What will I do?

Then he said (and I'm paraphrasing here), "but 80% when you're still experiencing chronic pain, doesn't feel like 80%. In fact, that's often why people regress. Their bodies and minds are spending so much time and energy dealing with the chronic pain that the original symptoms keep coming back."[14] You can't imagine my relief to have someone understand what I was going through.

I realized in that moment that traditional Western medicine had been minimizing my experiences, doubting my symptoms and their severity, and basically telling me to just get on with my life. To know that there was hope, was amazing. In response to the doctor, I said "it is such a shame that these therapies aren't widely known and that you really have to be your own advocate for your health. But at the same time, it's still wonderful that they exist."

---

[14] BioFlex Laser Therapy. (Personal Communication, 2018). https://bioflexlaser.com/

Life Lesson
Read a book

Even with the CBD oil and the progress I had made, I felt like I had reached about 80% of my recovery and then plateaued. You will probably notice a pattern of mine—when I don't know what to do, I read a book. I read Norman Doidge's The Brain's Way of Healing: Remarkable Discoveries and Recoveries from the Frontiers of Neuroplasticity.[15] The book revealed many alternative therapies, but one chapter interested me in particular: traumatic brain injuries. The book outlined how low-level infrared laser therapy can help initiate the healing process by stimulating circulation and cell regeneration. I had heard of it before but didn't realize it was the same therapy until the author mentioned healing injuries for racehorses. I had previously met a woman at the dog park that had laser therapy done for her dog's arthritis. She spoke wonders about its success. At this point, once again, I was willing to try anything. So, I looked up the doctor mentioned in the book and was surprised to find that he was in Toronto.

---

[15] Doidge, N. (2016). *The Brain's Way of Healing: Stories of Remarkable Recoveries and Discoveries*. New York, NY: Penguin.

Photo Credit: Caio Resende from Pexels

I did treatments for a few months, covered by my benefits, and saw immense improvement. My faith and trust in traditional Western medicine has diminished. I am the kind of person who would rather know the truth and be frustrated, than not know and follow blindly.

I am now terribly paranoid about hitting my head or even falling. One winter I was walking my dog and slipped on some ice. I didn't even hit my head, but when I landed on my bum it jarred my brain and I started to have symptoms yet again. I still need to be exceedingly careful, but I've made more improvement by researching and advocating for my own recovery. Am I glad I had these experiences? Yes, it changed many things for me and not always for the better. But I know things now I didn't before and will use them to my advantage and to my girls' advantage and hopefully they will learn from my experiences.

Life Lesson
If you hear it once, it's a coincidence

If you hear it multiple times, it's worth your attention. I learned about Irlen Syndrome from three different people in the same year, and the most recent person linked it directly to concussions. And I thought, "What is Irlen Syndrome and maybe I should be tested". Irlen Syndrome is a perceptual processing disorder. It affects the brain's ability to process visual information. Irlen Syndrome affects 55 percent of those with traumatic brain injuries or concussions. Irlen Syndrome is often treated with coloured overlays (plastic sheets that overlay paper) or with coloured lenses (called spectral filters). These tools selectively filter out bothersome light and reduce activity in the brain that is causing the symptoms.[16]

What are the symptoms? Well, I have been wearing the lenses off and on for a year now and I'm not popping ibuprofen every day, I'm not falling asleep with an ice pack behind my head every night, I'm not nearly as irritable (unless it's before my morning coffee!), and I have my concentration back. I am able to handle so much more and function without using shortcuts. I used to try and rest as much as possible so that when my girls came home, I would be there for them, but then was debilitated afterward. And

> *most of all, I'm not in pain all the time. You don't realize how much pain you're tolerating until it's gone.*
>
>
>
> Photo Credit: Marcia Allyn Luke

Between infertility, postpartum depression, and numerous concussions, what advice can I give?

- When you know something is wrong, don't let anyone tell you you're fine.
- Keep seeking out different professionals until you find the help you need.
- Sometimes you may feel like you're going crazy, but chances are someone else has experienced what

---

[16] Irlen. (1998). Retrieved April 13, 2021, from http://www.irlen.com/

you're going through. Find others that can help even just by listening.
- Keep track of what you're experiencing, those notes may come in handy.
- Be your own advocate, and an advocate for your children. Don't give up, especially on yourself.

Have I found the magic balance of nutrition, sleep, and exercise? Not even close…having two kids under six means you eat a great deal of pizza, chicken fingers, grilled cheese, and cereal. Do I want to do better? Yes, absolutely! It's a work in progress. You do the best you can with what you have at the time and you strive to do better. I think the problem is when you stop striving, stop challenging yourself, and stop learning. Your body has to last you your whole life and that life can be long and good or short and bad. Talk to people you trust, listen to your body, and pick up a book!

Chapter 7
It takes one to know one

Friends come in and out of your life and one of the hardest lessons that I've had to learn is that a friend who's come and gone isn't necessarily a bad thing. Everyone in your life is here to show you something. Some are in it for the long haul and some are just a blip on the radar. But they have come into your life for a purpose and instead of being sad and trying to hang on, be grateful.

Photo Credit: Stokpic from Pexels

All that being said, it doesn't mean that you shouldn't try to keep in touch with the special people in your life. But if it just doesn't happen, it's okay. I may have mentioned before that my dad frowned upon my large group of friends and the loyalty and dedication that I showed them.[17] He was probably trying to protect me and to pass along lessons that he had learned much like I'm doing right now. There are people you can trust, but make them prove it…and while it's prudent to give second chances, don't give too many.

This sounds well and good on paper, but what does it look like in reality? I've already woven a number of my friendships throughout these pages, but here are a few more (numbered for anonymity) and what I've learned from each of them.

---

[17] Neufeld, G., & Maté, G. (2019). *Hold On to Your Kids: Why Parents Need to Matter More Than Peers*. London, England: Vermilion, an imprint of Ebury Publishing.

Elementary & High School
Time spent is more important than what you do

I'm still in touch with a surprising number of people from elementary and high school. In fact, some of these I still call close friends to this day. The history that you have with people while growing up is formative. They know you in a way that no new friend will ever know you. These early friends tend to come into your life out of circumstance: they ride the same school bus, they are in your class, they live on your street. Even still, you are drawn to people who are the most like you. I was drawn to the people on my bus who would sit and read a book, for example. That doesn't mean that you don't interact with the others, but your lasting friendships are those with whom you have common interests.

Photo Credit: JackF

Elementary and high school can be somewhat traumatic. There are those that will bully others to make themselves feel better or achieve a certain level of popularity. I never aimed to be part of the popular crowd. I aimed to fly under the radar and have my close group of friends and that was about all. One of my early friends, let's call her 1, lived close enough for us to bike to each other's houses. Out of my core friends, she was one of two who had a 'broken' family, meaning that her parents were divorced and while she lived down the road most of the time, she visited her dad periodically. Mind you, of the remaining four in my core, I know of at least two more separations that occurred as time went on, including my own parents, so…

Number 1 and I were both good at school, loved books, and were involved in Girl Guides and drama. She loved music and would often be found singing and dancing in the hallways at school or on the bus. She was friends with many different groups of people and could 'travel' these groups quite easily. I think in part what makes us such good friends is that we always have good conversations. There was a level of respect and no matter what we did, we always had a good time.

Letters to My Hypothetical Children

I was always envious of the relationship she had with her parents though. She could really talk to them. They respected her and she respected them. She had no reason to lie about where she was going or what she was doing. Her ability to speak up and out wasn't always well-received though. My parents struggled to like 1 because she spoke her mind and teachers would call her belligerent. Having children of my own now, I would rather they speak up than not at all. Now 1 also has her own children and I find that I really value her opinion and parenting practice. Part of the reason for this is that I respected her relationship with her parents growing up, but she's also an elementary school teacher. So, she has the experiences to draw from, but also a wealth of knowledge. And, as further evidence, her kids are great kids.

Funny story about 1…on my 39th birthday, we decided to go out dancing. We went to a community centre that was supposed to be for ages 30 plus. It was more like 50 plus. But they were playing music, serving drinks, and had a good-sized dance floor. So, we danced and had a great time, just the two of us. I'm sure the others wondered what we were doing there and wanted nothing more than for us to leave, but it just goes to show you that the good friends are the ones you have a good time with no matter what. They are also the ones you can talk to about anything, the ones you admire, and the ones that engage in mutual respect.

Another of my friends in elementary school, 2, was another person that was friends with everyone. She was always around and always friendly, but my friendship with 2 didn't really blossom until we were adults. Number 2 is a connector, an idea person, and shares her energy wherever she goes. I knew her throughout most of elementary and some of high school. We crossed paths and had some friends in common. I lost track of her for a while during university, but reconnected by fluke at a very transitional time for both of us.

When the girls turned one, I wasn't quite ready to go back to a full-time job. I hired a nanny part-time and started doing some freelance work for an old employer. And then I happened to talk to 2. I don't remember which one of us reached out or how we came to have that one fateful conversation, but she was looking for help building a website, developing business cards, and other such things. It was perfect timing and we started working together. I would edit things for her, draft documents, manage her online profile, whatever she needed really. And that started our working relationship.

What makes 2 and I such good friends is that we believe in the same things, we have a similar career trajectory, and our skills complement each other. If we were a bookstore, she would be the storefront, the pretty displays, and the person who talks to the customers, and I would be shipping/receiving, stocking, marketing, systems, etc. We have amazing conversations that get us both motivated and we believe in the magic of the universe. She always says, "What you put out in the universe is what you get back".[18] And it's true. You just need to listen. She's the friend that no matter how long you've gone without talking, it seems like no time has passed at all—another measure of a good friend.

Number 3 is quiet, but feisty and would have my back in any situation. We have a great deal in common as well: we both took English at university, we both took the LSAT, and we both applied to law school, but didn't go. We would go on trips together, sometimes to a hot beach destination, sometimes on a road trip, sometimes just around the corner to a relaxing spa-type destination. Then

---

[18] D.M. Hamelinck. (Personal Communication, 2015).

our paths went in different directions, but I feel we understand each other in a unique way because we reflect certain parts of each other. Number 3 has seen me super drunk, super duper hungover, she's seen me at my best and worst and still sticks around.

Funny story about 3 when she lived in this one shady apartment building. We got into the elevator one night and this clearly sketchy guy comes into the elevator with a shopping cart. So now there's not very much room to move around and he's ranting to himself and doesn't look well at all. It was one of those moments where you honestly believe @#$%* might go down. I could feel the silent communication between 3 and myself, preparing for the worst. And let me tell you, I'm glad it was 3 that was in that elevator with me.

What makes us such good friends is that we accept each other, we're not afraid to talk about the nitty gritty, and at the end of the day, we can laugh about everything. I feel at home with 3 and I hope she feels the same way about me. She's a sister from another mister. My only wish is that she lived closer than three provinces away.

University
R.E.S.P.E.C.T.

I made it through elementary and secondary school with minimal emotional scarring, but really looked forward to university. I felt like it would be my place. And it was in many respects. I found other 'nerds' who loved books and English as much as I did. They say the friends that you make in university are the ones that will stay with you for the rest of your life. What they don't tell you is that because you came from a variety of places to begin with, you won't always live in close proximity. Though I guess that's true of anyone. I will say that my university friends were different in that they were friendships developed quickly and furiously. While elementary and high school had the luxury of developing with a slow burn.

Photo Credit: Pexels from Pixabay

My first friend in university was 4, because she was my roommate. She was quite different from me, but she was a perfect fit. She was outgoing, social, and generous. I spent much of my first two months of university in my room or in the cafeteria. I was homesick and nervous and the only time I left residence was to go to class. I mentioned that 4 had a TV and an open-door policy, so our room became the social hub of our house. She was also persistent, and she brought me out of my shell, it just took a bit of time. Finally, Halloween came and as discussed earlier in these pages, she was very persistent. What I didn't share earlier comes after the night of dancing, but before the horrible hangover. What made that night even more perfect began with us not finding a cab at the end of the night. We saw a limo parked down the street and number 4 somehow convinced a limo driver to take whatever money we all had left and drive us back to residence before picking up his client. Who gets a limo ride back to residence? We did! It was such a memorable experience and certainly not the only one I would have with 4.

In my third year of university, 4 decided she wanted to organize a trip to Daytona Beach, Florida. It was the ultimate spring break party scene. There were four cars of people, we drove down stopping in Myrtle Beach for a couple of nights, and then spent the rest of the week at Daytona Beach. We even took a day trip to Disney World for a day of non-alcoholic amusement and I got to meet Mickey Mouse. 4 was friends with me by circumstance, but we spent so much time throughout university, even living together off campus, that we formed a true friendship. She is smart, dedicated, outgoing, and always included me. She was happy to share anything of her own with her friends. She was the exact roommate I needed.

Through 4, I met 5 and we ended up living with 5 in third year. Number 5 was bubbly, fun, quirky, and caring. She embraced her individuality and encouraged others to do the same. She was a bit of a neat freak like me, we both had curly hair, and she showed a degree of interest in who I was that I hadn't experienced in a long time. She was also incredibly determined; she could see when I needed a nudge and when I really meant "no". And she respected my choice either way. And for that reason, we had an excellent time when we lived together.

Number 5 reminds me a great deal of 3 in many ways. She's not afraid to talk about the tough stuff but loves to have fun. The last time we got together with our kids for a sleepover, we had a living room dance party and it was a blast. Even now when we're both parents, we're still having a good time. She's an instigator, but in the best possible way.

I remember after 5 had her first baby, she was exhausted and dealing with her son's severe case of diaper rash. I went to help because I didn't want to be one of those friends who's all talk. But I didn't have kids and I didn't know what to do to help her. She was breastfeeding so I couldn't do that. I couldn't change diapers because it was a process involving a hair dryer to make sure the baby's bum was completely dry. So, I ended up going grocery shopping and making dinner. I felt helpless, but I hope that my help was better than nothing. I certainly felt when I had my own babies that any help provided was a gift and I think having the company and spending that time together made our friendship stronger.

Number 6 was another friend that I met through 4 and while we didn't live together, we spent a lot of time together during university, but even after. Number 6 is one of the most caring, kind, and selfless people that I know. After university, I lived in North York and 6 and I would get together to watch our favourite show, *Gilmore*

Girls. I remember when I saw the last episode of the series, I had no idea it was the end of the entire show. After it was over, something clicked, and I immediately called 6 to commiserate over the end. Years later they did a reboot and we got together to watch that as well. She had custom mugs made for us.

Number 6 and I are both a bit nerdy, a little quirky, and appreciate each other's company. I had the honour of being in her wedding party, I remember all the incredibly useful tips she gave me about being a twin mom, and she always makes an effort to get together. She goes above and beyond to let you know that she's your friend and inspires you to do the same in return.

Number 7 was actually someone I knew from elementary school, but didn't really start hanging out with regularly until university. In high school we sometimes crossed paths or social circles, but not that often really. We were two of very few that had gone to Guelph and he had a truck so I would carpool home with him on the weekends. Number 7 became a close friend because we had enough history to be completely honest and sometimes that's what you need when you're in university and homesick. You need someone that's familiar with all the same things and people that you are. We lost touch after university for awhile. Then one day I saw his old truck on the highway and I reached out. We are still good friends to this day and his lovely wife has become a very welcome addition to our friend group.

Work
Avoid office politics and place your trust carefully

Work is a whole other ball game when it comes to friends. You should take your time to get to know people and decide whether they can be trusted outside of work. Since there are politics involved, you don't want to trust someone too soon and accidentally commit a career limiting move. That being said, some of my besties have come from work.

Photo Credit: Fauxels from Pexels

Number 8 is boisterous, vulgar, loud, and awesome. I took a chance with 8 because she told me that her friend was experiencing fertility issues and I was at the time too. I really wanted to talk to her friend and I opened up to 8. I had kept my own fertility issues pretty quiet at work, but felt that I could trust 8. I wasn't sorry. She put me in touch with her friend and was very understanding. That started a bananas awesome friendship. We worked well together, had the same philosophies, and could call it like it was which sometimes sucked. Even after leaving that place of work, we have stayed friends.

8 has twin daughters as well, though they are several years older than mine. When my girls were quite little, 8 convinced me to bring them to her family's farm for a swim. That was their first swim ever. We had a great time dipping the girls in the pool (she held one for me of course), showing them the horses, and throwing a ball for the dog.

Number 9 is professional, down to earth, and always realistic. We worked closely together and that was how our friendship formed. We worked well, released some incredible products, and had fun doing it all. I went to her wedding at 35 weeks pregnant with twins (thank goodness for the maternity section at Target) where she was married to a good friend of the girls' dad. She has high ideals, works hard, and loves to laugh.

My favourite time with 9 was when we went to Quebec City for a work conference. The weather was beautiful, and we walked all around the city just talking and getting to know each other better. It was kind of like the first date of friendships. You tentatively ask questions, hoping not to offend, learning more about each other, and tallying up common interests and viewpoints.

Number 10 is smart, calls it like it is, and feisty. She's a true feminist, but a scrappy one. She will always give you her honest opinion. 10 and I worked on several projects together, but also had the pleasure of co-chairing a leadership group. We ran workshops, organized a book club, had an annual event with guest speakers, and generally helped people get the most out of and for their careers. She's always been a huge supporter of mine (as I am of her) and we are still helping each other out in both career and life. She knows she's not perfect and is willing to admit it and tends to see the best in others.

I actually happen to live right around the corner from 10 currently. We sometimes meet at the park with our kids or go for a walk without our kids. Before the COVID-19 pandemic, we would go for lunch or to a patio for drinks; during the pandemic, we've stuck to front lawn visits. It's nice knowing she's just around the corner.

Infertility & PPMD
Sometimes good things come from hitting rock bottom

I mentioned previously that I struggled with infertility and postpartum depression. These were some of the most difficult times I have ever been through. I tentatively started talking to people about infertility and found there were more people struggling with it than I previously thought. And talking about it seemed to help a great deal. When the postpartum depression hit, I did the same thing. Some people understood and talked about their own experiences. Some people didn't understand, but they were respectful. These experiences helped me see the power of storytelling in a different way.

Photo Credit: Anemone123 from Pixabay

One of my 'rock bottom' friends is the wife of someone I know from high school, number 11. She is a talker, and she fires questions off like a firing range. You think that she hasn't even heard the answer to the first question when she's on the second and third. But you will be surprised, she pays attention and will bring up things that you forget yourself. She's kind and intelligent and loving. She has no problem sharing her failures and successes and she understands people very intuitively. We are good friends, because we want the same things in life: to do something meaningful with our skills, be good parents, and enjoy time with friends and family. We talk about books and world issues. She's also the hostess with the 'mostess', making excellent food and conversation. The shared grief and sorrow of infertility is something that you have to experience to fully understand. Through this shared experience, we formed a deep connection. I actually dated her husband when I was younger, so they are a friendship tag team of sorts. He's the kind of friend that you can just sit in silence or say anything and it's all good. He's the kind of friend that would be there for you no matter what…and I think we have been there for each other through all of the big things in life. I honestly talk with his wife more now, but together they are an unstoppable force in friendship.

Numbers 12 and 13 were friends I met at the dog park (or because of dogs) and both lived close to me at the time. We lost touch around the time that I had the girls, but I reconnected with both…at a postpartum support group, of all places. Once again, the experience of hitting rock bottom and being able to talk about it in a non-judgemental space was the first step to overcoming. We would take our kids to the park or to the mall in the winter (before the stores opened) and let them run around. There were three adults against four children. We would help with each other's children and with some understanding company it seemed not as overwhelming. We would let the kids run around and then when they wore themselves out, we would pop them in their strollers, give them a snack, and walk until they fell asleep. That was when we got our time to talk. They were going through the same thing, so there was that amazing depth of understanding and connection. We called ourselves the 'sad mommies' group', but it was so much more than that. These women became part of my 'tribe'; the strong, real women that will stand up for you and with you with ferocity (also see below 'Love is all you need' regarding one's tribe).

Twins & Triplets
Shared experiences create deep connections

With every major life transition, I have found another meaningful element of myself, filling the gaps that I didn't know I had. My parents of multiples group was just that—something in my life that I didn't know was missing. I was looking forward to having twins and I knew it was going to be difficult. But there are things that only your twin and triplet friends understand.

Photo Credit: Marcia Allyn Luke

Here are just a few of the tips and tricks I learned from parents of multiples:

- Don't worry about being the "perfect" mom; count the wins, not the so-called losses.

- Sleep when the baby sleeps. Everyone will tell you this…actually do it though!
- Other than food, shelter, and relative cleanliness, love is all you need. What makes them feel loved and what makes you feel loved? That's all you need, end of story. Anything else is a bonus.
- Keep a playpen with a change station in the living room so you don't have to go upstairs for every changing or nap.
- Keep onesies and sleepers in the living room in baskets for easy clothing changes. And don't even bother putting them in real clothes for the first while.
- Do powdered formula (if you decide to do formula) and use room temperature water so that the babies are used to it and you can mix easily on the go.
- After every bottle, run a full kettle and let it cool between feedings, so you have sterile water for the next time.
- Put the bottles in the dishwasher on the hottest setting. It sterilizes them (even if there are other foods) and then let them dry on a drying rack. It might not be exactly the same, but it was close enough.

- Wash everything together and if it stains, it stains. Avoid white or light colours. If it doesn't survive the dryer, it wasn't meant to be.
- Forget the wipe warmer (unless you have an infant with horrible diaper rash), you don't want to get the babies used to that luxury. It's an extra step and when you do it six to 10 times a day, you want it to be fast. You also won't have the wipe warmer when you're on the go, so if you get them used to the lowest common denominator there are no unrealistic expectations.
- Sleepers with zippers (so much easier in the middle of the night and when you are overtired) and onesies that snap up the front (so that you don't have to pull a poopy onesie over the baby's head).[19]

The first parents of multiples event that I ever attended was at my house. Most of these events didn't start until 8pm and I was usually so tired that I just went to bed. If I hosted one though, then I had to attend and I was so glad that I did. I looked around the room and just listened to

---

[19] Luke, M. A. (2021, February 18). Throwback Thursday: The Quick and Dirty. Retrieved February 18, 2021, from www.twinhorseshoes.ca/2021/02/17/throwback-thursday-the-quick-and-dirty

the conversation. These people had the same challenges I had, they took the same shortcuts, they weren't horrible moms so that meant I wasn't either. I felt relieved, normal, and accepted as a mom for the first time. It almost brought tears to my eyes.

One of my best twin mom friends, 14 is one of the kindest people I know, and she doesn't judge. I met 14 because she was collecting items for less fortunate families. I didn't sell my baby stuff once I was done with it…we were fortunate to receive a tonne of hand-me-downs and so I felt it was only fair to donate my items once I was finished. I would come and drop off some things and 14 would make me coffee and that's how we got to know each other. We were both part of the same multiples group and volunteered to help with many things over the years. We always made time for our friendship. I think our shared experience as twin moms was an important start to our friendship.

Harry Potter
Fandom creates a unique shared language

I joke frequently that any life lesson, any challenging situation, has an answer inside the pages of the Harry Potter series.[20] I've read them multiple times, I've watched the movies multiple times, I've been to plays, amusement parks, and other exhibits devoted to the wizarding world of Harry Potter. It's a language that I understand and oddly enough, some others do as well.

Photo Credit: Marcia Allyn Luke

I met number 15 through her husband, who I worked with at the time. Shortly after I met 15, her husband left the company I worked for, which was the catalyst to keep in

---

[20] Rowling, J.K. (2018). *Harry Potter* (Series). London, England: Bloomsbury.

touch. 15 and I had an instant connection and while there are many levels to our friendship, our initial connection was forged through *Harry Potter*, though we also enjoy *Outlander*.[21] Our first solo friend date was to the Ontario Science Centre where they had a display of many of the props and costumes used in the Harry Potter films. It was fantastic and we started hanging out on our own more often. 15 is super creative, artistic, and bubbly. She has a child-like quality that keeps everyone around her young at heart.

15 falls into the infertility friend group as well. She had difficulties getting pregnant and this was another area for us to bond and support each other. About five months after she had her eldest daughter, we took a trip to Orlando to go to Universal Studios and see the Wizarding World of Harry Potter. We could have walked around looking at the shops and the castle all day long. Never mind the rides and the merchandise and shows. It was amazing. We did spend some time in the rest of Universal Studios. It was October or November, it was about 20 degrees Celsius, and we made the colossal mistake of doing a water ride midday thinking that we would dry out. Not so much. We

---

[21] Gabaldon, D. (1991). *Outlander* (Series). New York, NY: Delacorte.

ended up at a shop buying pajama pants so that we wouldn't freeze. We were like little kids in a candy store the whole time. I genuinely believe that 15 is my soul sister. We were put on this earth to support and help each other. Through 15, I understand that someone in life that is not related by blood can actually be a part of your family.

Camryn & Maya
Love is all you need

I have met so many people through the simple act of having children. And I have shared love for these girls with so many others. Some people are in your life to be part of your 'tribe' (by which I mean your core group of friends and family that will be there for you no matter what). Some people are there to share the heart-bursting moments. Some people are there to let you know that you're normal. Some people are there to love your kids when you aren't there to do so, either physically or emotionally. I'm still learning all the wonderful ways that friends and family are capable of love and support (and what I can provide in return). These girls have made that world of possibility so much bigger with their presence.

Photo Credit: Marcia Allyn Luke

Number 16 was one of the girls' teachers at their preschool. She was the only teacher that the girls would go to willingly and especially when they were upset. They would find her wherever she was in the school. Thank goodness it was a small building. I jokingly asked her one day as she helped me take the girls to the car, whether she would be interested in babysitting them or if that would be a conflict of interest. She was totally willing, and she became the only person other than family to watch the girls in those early days. She told me once that she didn't know it was possible to love someone else's children as much as she loved Cami and Maya. It made my heart feel like it would burst.

'Miss' 16 would come by to see the girls, even when she wasn't babysitting, and we became friends. Eventually, we started hanging out even when the girls weren't home. Even though there's almost 10 years difference between us, 16 is an old soul (and hopefully I'm a young one too) and we often forget the age difference. Until I mention a movie that she's never heard of or we realize that she was in elementary school when I was in university. When she was stuck for a place to live, she moved in with the girls and me. When the girls were with their dad, we would walk to the local pub and have drinks and appetizers, then walk back home. On one of these walks home, we both had to pee. Both of us are country girls, so we picked a somewhat side street and did our business. Never mind, the fact that we were in a busy subdivision and a few cars beamed their headlights on our bared bums. When you gotta go, you gotta go. She's become a part of the family and I hope she always will be.

The Golden Rule

It really is: "treat others the way you want to be treated"

I haven't always been the best kind of friend. I've been selfish at times, angry at others, taken some friends for granted, shut other ones out. Most of the times that I haven't been a good friend also coincide with when I was struggling with mental health, but I didn't always realize this myself so couldn't articulate it to others. I'm not proud of how I've been as a friend at various points in my life, but the qualities that I am proud of are these:

- *Dropping anything to help a friend in need.*
- *Following through on commitments.*
- *Sharing what I have with friends.*
- *Being honest.*
- *Giving heartfelt advice.*
- *Listening attentively.*
- *Being the one to make plans with someone.*
- *Making people smile or laugh.*
- *Pointing out the good qualities in someone.*
- *Giving real hugs.*

Photo Credit: Helena Lopes from Pexels

I always asked people about relationships, "how do you know when you meet THE ONE?" and the answer was always, "you just know" which I found irritating. I think the same response applies to friends, but I'll try to expand on the answer. I've learned that friends treat you the way that you should be treated and that you can tell a lot from how someone treats other people first. They will call you on your @#$%* rather than just telling you what you want to hear because they want the best for you. They will have the difficult conversations, but in a respectful way. They don't judge and they don't betray the trust you give them. They spend time with you doing something or doing nothing, but they are comfortable to be around. But most of all, I've learned that true friends are the ones that you want to be a good friend to, the ones that the effort doesn't seem like work…because you care.

There is something about a friend that you will recognize even if you've never met them before, as long as you're paying attention. This chapter is called, "It takes one to know one" because there's something that's reflected from your soul back to theirs and vice versa. A soulmate doesn't have to be a romantic partner—the best friends in life are soulmates too.

Chapter 8
What doesn't kill you makes you stronger

Clichés become cliches for a reason, because they are used so frequently that they somehow lose meaning or sincerity. Here are just a few examples:
- *What doesn't kill you makes you stronger.*
- *Life wouldn't give you something you can't handle.*
- *You can't appreciate the good, until you've experienced the bad.*

But cliches started out with a measure of truth. It's about the timing in which they are delivered. Sometimes you can stand back and appreciate these words objectively, maybe even take comfort from them. If you're in crisis mode, maybe you can't. It's a good thing we have cliches though because sometimes there are no other words to offer in times of crisis.

Times of trial show you who you are, they confront you in a way that it's almost impossible for you not to learn. And if you don't learn it the first time, you will continue to be challenged until you do. The universe just knocks a little louder and a little louder until you get it through your skull.

Photo Credit: Maryam62 from Pixabay

My family wasn't exactly the most open when it came to emotions and communication. When I grew up, self-regulation wasn't a term I heard. I controlled my emotions and that was how I managed them. Sometimes they leaked out unexpectedly. When I was a kid, I would get super angry and then cry. That's just how it would come out. Then I learned about the joy of slamming things or hitting things, which wasn't especially healthy either, but at least most often they were inanimate objects. Because I didn't know what to do with my emotions, I trusted my brain instead. This is a very responsible way to make decisions, but it's not always accurate. That's in part what this chapter is about. If you can learn to listen to yourself and tap into your emotions, you're better equipped to make decisions using both your heart and your head.

Life Lesson
Love hurts

One of the first emotional struggles I remember was when my sister was diagnosed with Crohn's disease. She was 15 and they thought it was appendicitis. When she got to the hospital and they opened her up, they found out that it wasn't appendicitis and they transferred her to Sick Kid's Hospital. It was extremely scary for me. I was 12 and was lucky in that this type of emergency hadn't really happened in my life yet. It was one of those times when I knew my parents were worried. My dad started to cry when he told me where my sister was and what was happening. We were in the car on the way to the hospital. My dad never cried. Then I saw her in the hospital bed with tubes in her nose and a huge incision in her stomach, the nurses were helping her with a bed pan, and we spent Christmas in the hospital. It was horrible for me, but I can't even imagine what it was like for my sister. That's one of the ways you know you love someone, when it hurts you to see them hurting.

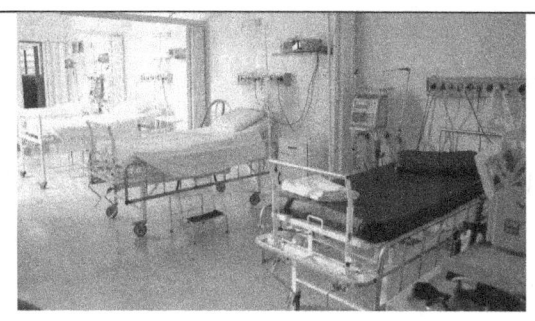
Photo Credit: 1662222 from Pixabay

I was quiet, I wanted people to like me, and had grown up pushing down my feelings, which meant I sometimes did things that I didn't want to do. Don't get me wrong, I wasn't succumbing to peer pressure in life-or-death situations. But I did seek out attention from boys in an unhealthy way. My dad was always distant with me—he was great on family vacations or camping, but in day-to-day life he was usually working. My dad would typically be out in the garage working on someone's car or he would be cutting the grass. He had a hard time sitting still. He and I had quite different personalities as well, so I was constantly striving to get attention, whether positive or negative.

I only realized this years later, of course, when I finally put the pieces together. I chased relationships that were unhealthy because I was recreating the 'chasing' dynamic with my dad. Now, I'm no psychologist and I'm not saying that my dad and I had a dysfunctional relationship, but I realize now how impactful my childhood experiences were. In translation, I craved attention, good or bad, from boys regardless of whether I liked them or not.

Another significant factor in my emotional development was my family's relationships. My parents met when my mom was 15 and married at 18; my sister and brother-in-law met when she was 15 and while they took their time getting married, they are still together today. This was my frame of reference for relationships and marriage. I thought I would meet my future husband in high school and every time it didn't happen, I was devastated. I wasn't shopping for the right person, I kept assuming that the next relationship would be the right one. I'm sure you can see at this point how these factors are a dangerous combination of perceptions and expectations: daddy issues, seeking attention, and an expectation of meeting my future husband in high school.

The bottom line is I had sex younger than I probably should have, though not as early as some of my friends.

Thankfully, I was smart enough to use protection, but many in my high school ended up pregnant—about 12 in our grade alone. The high school built a daycare on site and it was supposed to be for the community and for those interested in teaching or ECE to get experience, but really it was a way to keep these girls in school.

Now, to go back to 'pushing down feelings'…in my opinion, ignoring your feelings is probably the most dangerous thing that you can teach your children, especially girls. If young people push down their feelings and ignore their inner voice in some situations, they will self-doubt every time they have those feelings. We tell children that they are in control of their bodies, but then we take them to the doctor and say "now take off your clothes and let the doctor touch you" even though they are a stranger. If children have to tolerate unwanted touching in some cases, how are they equipped to differentiate between acceptable and unacceptable situations?

I know in my case, I trusted my logical brain, my friends, a magazine article, pretty much anything except my feelings. And it's not just the listening to feelings part that is important. I think children need to be able to articulate these feelings too, so that when the time comes they can say "no" with confidence. Because there will be a time that they will have to say "no", and I don't want my girls to second guess or have self-doubt. This applies to sex, alcohol, drugs, getting into a car with someone who's inebriated, jumping off a bridge, vandalism, theft, violence, bullying, etc.

Children need to know ahead of time how to listen to their inner voice, how to articulate their feelings confidently. Think about it. We have fire drills in school, so kids know what to do in case of a real fire. But we don't rehearse how to say no to someone pressuring our kid to have sex? We don't rehearse how to say no to alcohol or drugs? We don't rehearse kids walking away and calling their parents at any time to come home?

We're starting to rehearse what to say when bullying happens, but it had to reach the point where kids were dying first. Even 'stranger danger' could use a little more in the sense of practical role play. They aren't just going to pull up and ask a kid to get in the vehicle. They are going to say, "hey, I have puppies at home, do you want to come and see them?" or "your mom told me to pick you up, I work with her". Let's not leave it to chance.

Life Lesson
The birds and the bees

The thing about having sex the first time is that you can't take it back. I immediately started worrying that my boyfriend at the time would leave me. I had sex with him because I honestly thought we were going to get married. But it opened the door to more insecurities than I ever thought possible. That should have been my first clue. If it's the right person, you shouldn't feel insecure about it afterwards. And it's not just the first time that you have sex that you can't take back (though it's maybe the most important), it's your first time with anyone. And if I hadn't been smart and used protection, I hypothetically might have been tied to that person for the rest of my life, either with a child or a sexually transmitted infection (STI). To put it in perspective, this is someone that I haven't spoke with since high school. And just because you have had sex, doesn't mean the next person gets to pick up where the last one left off. It's not a free pass for anyone to claim anything. It's always your decision and that should never be questioned.

Now let me tell you about how my first time could have been different. I was dating a boy that I liked an awful lot and somehow managed to get to his house. We were unsupervised (except for the tenant in his mom's basement), we were drinking, and we tried to have sex that night. Because we were drunk it wasn't successful (thank goodness), but it was also because we were drunk that we thought it was a good idea (big mistake). We weren't prepared, we didn't have protection, and the tenant from the basement, who was probably in his 20s, kept walking in on us (weird and not at all coincidental which is more than scary looking back). Now how many ways could that situation have gone wrong? And if it had actually been my first time, instead of with someone I loved, what impact would that have had on me? What if that older guy decided to crash the party (so to speak) and turn two's company into three's a crowd? Would the guy I was dating have been in any position to do anything to stop him?

I could have been raped that night, that could have been my first experience. I was 15 and I messed up big that night. Why was I even there in the first place? Because I lied to my parents. I was lucky, but how many girls aren't? How many girls are careful and aware of what's going on and still end up being assaulted or raped? What I did, putting myself in that vulnerable situation, is disrespectful to myself and to other girls and women who have been victimized.

Photo Credit: Bibhukalayan Acharya from Pexels

After my first serious boyfriend and I broke up after two years and giving my virginity to him, I was devastated (not losing my virginity, the term 'losing' indicates both that it was a loss that I should grieve and that I'm of lesser value as a person afterward). My parents liked him. He was smart, good looking, confident. His parents did well in life. I thought, what's wrong with me, how did I screw this up? My self-esteem took a big hit. And then I went out with a guy that I didn't know very well. Sort of a friend of a friend. And it was okay at first, we had fun. But he drank an awful lot and I started to get uncomfortable. More than once I was mopping up beer and cleaning up broken beer bottles with his mom. Him and his brother would get into fights in the living room, and I started to fear getting caught up in the physical violence.

He was a virgin, so he was eager to have sex and I thought "well, what difference does it make at this point…the damage is already done." So, I had sex with him. But it eventually became apparent to me that I didn't want to be with this person anymore. It took a while, and my inner voice was pretty much shouting by the time I listened. One night, he wanted to have sex and I didn't. Instead of saying no, I didn't say anything. I distinctly remember trying to push him off of me and he pushed back. It was enough to make me afraid; I didn't say anything more, I let myself down.

And after, I broke up with him. I don't remember what I said, but it wasn't easy. He became somewhat stalker-like. I didn't really give him a good reason for breaking up, but I also should have realized that I didn't need one. I actually don't remember much about the six months of time during and after that breakup. The smell of beer became traumatic for me and I hated being around drunk people, but more specifically guys. My skin crawled when I was in crowds, and when people got too close to me, especially guys that were much bigger than me. I shut down and withdrew for some time and any inquiries from my friends were met with hostility and defensiveness.

Parenting Perspective
Make sure you don't wait to have the sex talk

Don't wait for your kids to ask questions. Chances are they will find out information from another source and never ask their parents. Don't keep putting it off because it's uncomfortable. Don't gloss over it because it's awkward. And don't leave out the emotions. Use your own personal experience. It might be difficult to remember but go back in your mind and your heart and dig up those feelings because those will inspire your child to believe you and trust you. Be honest because chances are, they've already heard more at school or read more online than you know. Unfortunately, kids are having sex younger and younger and whether that's a result of exposure to online content that's more mature than it should be at their age, or hormones in our food, or any combination of other factors...it's not going to stop just because you refuse to have the talk. Your children don't need your permission or advice to have sex. Talk to them before it gets to that point, so that at least they are making an informed decision.

My almost first time and my actual first time both happened before my parents had the sex talk with me. I believe I was already on the birth control pill when my parents (my mom) had the sex talk with me. As a side note, I also had a certain proclivity for walking in on people having sex (yuck). But I don't think this made me any more curious than any other teenager.

Photo Credit: Couleur from Pixabay

For some reason, I always had it in my head that I didn't want to try drugs. Maybe because alcohol was good enough and I didn't want to push the limit. Maybe because I saw examples of those who did drugs around me and I didn't like what I saw. I also knew that drinking and driving was a no-fly zone. These were my limits and not because of my parents. I made these decisions myself and because I believed in them strongly and made the choice myself, I stuck to them. But the same conversation goes for alcohol and drugs. Don't wait until it's too late. Come prepared with enough information that you are a credible source in your children's eyes. And be honest.

I eventually surfaced from the fog a bit, but was still cautious. All of this happened during my OAC year of high school and not that long before going away to university. I feel it also explains in part why I was so reluctant to go out to the bar in university. I didn't want to be left alone and I didn't really trust drunk dudes.

In fact, the first guy I dated after starting university didn't drink at all. I realize it's a stereotype, but he wasn't a 'guy's guy' (meaning that he wasn't a big guy, or a loud guy, or an aggressive sports guy, etc.). He was small enough that one Halloween he squeezed into my jeans for part of his cowboy costume. He was musical, vegetarian, and fun. We would go out to the bar and he would dance just as much as I would. It was fantastic.

For me all of this also meant that he was completely non-threatening, which allowed me to trust him more easily. We dated for three years, lived together for two of those, and had two cats together. When I got my job in North York, we found out that we didn't want the same things. He didn't want to live in Toronto and I wanted to pursue my career there. We had a great connection, but not a shared vision of the future. It was a sad, but mutual break up and we are still friends to this day.

I guess you could say that I figured out how to listen to my voice the hard way. But it could have been much, much worse. What if I had stayed with the rebound guy? What if he had gotten violent? What if I had responded in the opposite way, purposely putting myself into dangerous situations as a big F-you to the world. Part of me wanted to, I'm not going to lie. What if I had started abusing substances to deal with my feelings? That could open up a whole bunch of other dangerous situations. What if I never learned to listen to my feelings? I also realize now that listening is an ongoing process, so stay tuned.

Getting back to my parents…I thought they had a good marriage. If you remember, we used to call my mom 'June Cleaver'. She wasn't quite part of that generation, but my parents held very traditional roles. My mom was not necessarily subservient to my dad, but he 'wore the pants' so to speak. I watched her cater to him to a large extent early on. When she went back into the workforce, her individuality and independence started to grow, but that was much later. I never thought, in a million years, that they would split up after over 40 years of marriage. That day will forever be cemented in my mind.

My mom and sister came over and we were sitting on my back deck. And my mom started to talk. There were tears and hugs, shock and sadness. For the first time in my life, I realized I had anxiety (this also helped me make the connection to my childhood anxiety). It felt like someone was sitting on my chest and I couldn't get enough air. At the same time, I was about to go in for IVF and ended up postponing it because I didn't want the stress to sabotage the chances of success. I had already been through the ringer with miscarriages and infertility. I needed some time to bounce back.

For my mom, I immediately went into action mode. We went one night when we knew my dad wouldn't be home, loaded my car to the top and she came to live with me while we searched for an apartment. She was rocked, but she was also empowered. I was extremely proud of her for doing what she needed to in order to be happy. After the initial shock wore off, I began analyzing my whole childhood. Was any of it real? What was I striving for if not? What was the new standard (if it existed) by which I should judge my own relationship? How could you ever trust anyone? I focused on the differences between my parents' relationship and my own instead of looking for the similarities. I also decided that even though my parents were no longer together, that didn't necessarily invalidate my memories of my childhood.

The girls' dad and I went ahead with IVF a few months later, and it was successful. We were over the moon. Dealing with infertility, IVF, and then a twin pregnancy, all wreaked havoc on my body. My hormones surging off and on with every miscarriage, then adding simulated hormones to increase egg production, and then off charts with twins. Which meant that they dropped just as hard or worse afterwards. You're more likely to have PPMD with both fertility treatments and twins, so I should have known. But it came as a surprise.

I had never had depression (unless you count the sullen teenage version, which I don't). It was extremely difficult to cope with PPMD and newborn twins who ended up developing acid reflux. It made it exceedingly difficult to bond with the girls and I still think I've blocked out the baby experience that so many parents seem to enjoy. Much of the time I felt like I was looking after someone else's kids. Sometimes I was angry. Sometimes I would just check out and play on my phone. Sometimes I would cry, sometimes a lot. I felt like a horrible mother and a horrible person.

Post-partum depression made me question the stereotypes and expectations we put on new parents. You know the ones. The rose-coloured glasses, mom gazing lovingly into the baby's eyes, carrying the baby in a sling everywhere she goes, not being able to leave her baby with anyone else. I had an idea these were fake, but to experience it is something else. I was lucky I had lots of help and friends who were going through it too. My whole outlook changed though. I didn't have the time or energy to pretend. Sometimes, I wore the same clothes three days in a row, day and night, and couldn't find time or energy to shower. I learned not to judge anyone—I wouldn't want anyone to judge me based on my first 18 months of motherhood. Everyone has a story that you don't know about so give them the benefit of the doubt.

I also realized that I didn't believe the illusion anymore, the glossy perfect one perpetuated by media. So many things had happened that I didn't expect and my way of coping before was always to believe it happened for a reason. Well, this time it did. The reason was for me to reset my expectations of myself and others, to see the world for what it really was, and to connect with people in a different way that was honest and real, and sometimes messy. This was clearly very contradictory to how I was raised and how I'd lived life so far.

It literally took changing everything in my life to realize what I needed. And it really took hitting rock bottom for the message to get through. We had moved with the girls to this amazing country home with property and character, I had changed my job completely, I should have been blissful. But I wasn't. I was at the point where I felt the girls would be better off without me, that I couldn't imagine continuing to live feeling the way I was feeling.

I was hopeless and felt so much pain and I couldn't describe why. I realize now that I was living contrary to my heart/soul/purpose, whatever you want to call it. I finally saw that my marriage was the only piece of the puzzle I hadn't examined. My vision of my future life had changed, my faith in the institution of marriage was fragile at best, and the trust between the two of us, after everything we had been through, was gone. We were exceptionally good at the business of life, but at the expense of our relationship.

Life Lesson
If you want real change, you have to tear down the castle

If the change is big enough, you can't just add on and patch things up. I had been adding and patching for many years. But my foundation had been shaken and cracked, my vision of what I wanted had done a 180, and I realized that I couldn't just keep doing home improvements and moving to different houses. The castle had to be torn down and rebuilt, one brick at a time.

I will say that the hard work for me has always been leading up to any major decision. I go back, soul search, ask the tough questions, examine from all angles, cry and scream, consider all possibilities, 'try them on' so to speak, and by the time the decision is made, I'm at peace with it. Much of this goes on behind the scenes, so from the outside it might look like I'm making heavy decisions lightly. But really, it's been torture. Eventually, you have to do the hard work—for some people it comes after the decision.

Photo Credit: Lisa Fotios from Pexels

The silver lining is that the girls' dad and I had two beautiful girls together, we get along now better than we ever have, and we co-parent quite well. Now I've had the opportunity to see both of my parents with new partners and I've seen the resiliency and hard work involved in my sister's marriage. I haven't always gotten along with my brother-in-law. He and my sister used to fight a lot when they were younger and I didn't think she was happy. But they turned a corner, and it wasn't without effort, but they have an excellent relationship. My brother-in-law has been there for all the big stuff, good and bad, and he still sticks around. More importantly my sister is still with him and that says an awful lot about his character in my mind. They say anything worth having is worth fighting for, which I think is true for them both.

I've seen my family in some of the worst times, rise to the challenge and come to my rescue. My parents were in the middle of a separation and divorce, but when I needed help with my newborn babies and postpartum depression they were there. No questions were asked, I had help at every feeding to help manage the girls' acid reflux. My dad surprised me the most; he was so good with the girls even in those early days. He is the kind of grandpa now for my girls that I always wanted him to be as my dad. I'm not resentful about this, in fact, I am so grateful to see this side of him and to watch him and my daughters enjoy each other's company. It has expanded our sometimes-challenging relationship yet again and given it room to grow.

I've watched my mom become a grandma for my girls. I know how close I was with Grams and I see that they have and will have that relationship with her. And yet my mom still has the ability and fortitude to 'mother' me when I need it the most. She will always be the matriarch; my mom holds the wisdom, the heart, and the soul of our family. My sister, who doesn't have kids of her own but is an 'Aunt' to many of her friends' children, has a special place in the heart of my daughters. I hope they see in her the sister that I've always cherished. I hope they see in her husband the brother-in-law that I've come to realize is as solid as a rock. And finally, I hope they have with each other a fraction of the wonderful memories that I have with my sister. Here are just a few:

- My sister doing my hair for me when I was little. She would pull so hard, but it would be the smoothest ponytail ever and would last all day long, even if it did give me a headache from being too tight.
- Going to Canada's Wonderland every summer with my mom, aunt, and grandma. My favourite memories were when I was finally tall enough to ride the big roller coasters with my sister.
- Riding around in my sister's Camaro, listening to music, and being teenagers together. Except for that one time when I locked her keys in the car. Oops!
- My sister's wedding. It is still one of the best weddings I've attended. The hotel went out and purchased a barbeque for her wedding because she wanted her favourite food, hamburgers.
- Any time that we went out dancing or hung out together. One more than memorable experience was when we introduced my mom to test tube shooters on her 50th birthday. We played games and had a great time. And have had many of these nights since.

Families aren't perfect, any of them. And if you think they are, start looking because there are likely secrets to be found. But a family doesn't have to be perfect to teach you about life. And you don't have to be perfect to live it; you are whether you do it intentionally or not. I've started rebuilding my castle. It will take a while for it to be complete. I will be re-evaluating its structure probably for the rest of my life, making sure that it's what I want and that I don't stop listening to my inner voice again. I have always believed that there are no mistakes or regrets. Everything I've done in my life has led me to where I am and when I found I didn't like my life, I would evaluate and change my path. The things that haven't killed me have certainly made me stronger. These challenges in life aren't accidental, they are meant to help guide you through life. They are also meant to remind you who you are and what you can do. I truly believe that if you listen to and learn from your experiences (or the experiences of others), you'll never have any regrets in life.

Epilogue
Dear Cami and Maya

What else can I say? I'm still learning and making so-called mistakes. I'm still trying to manage my emotions. Sometimes I'm too easy going and sometimes I lose my mind over nothing. I can be an all or nothing kind of person and that comes with its downfalls. I would like to live a more balanced life, but at the same time I love the passion with which I attack everything I do. Most of all, I would like to be able to answer that timeless question, why are we all here? What is the purpose of life? What happens after we die? I'm not sure anyone is ever able to answer these questions absolutely. We might be lucky enough to find the answers for ourselves, but that doesn't mean they apply to everyone.

Cami and Maya, I hope that I can learn from you as much as you learn from me. I hope that we always have the kind of relationship where we can talk about anything. I hope you learn these lessons faster and better than I did, but regardless you'll figure it out and I'll be there along the way. Most of all, I hope that you are safe, healthy, happy, and successful (whatever that means to you). And don't stop trying, ever. If I did, I wouldn't have both of you.

Love Always, Mom

A Case of the Sillies

I feel the most like your mom when we are being silly. It's one of the best ways I have of connecting with you both. I hope that you feel the same way.

Photo Credit: Marcia Allyn Luke

Photo Credit: Marcia Allyn Luke

Acknowledgements
Twin Horseshoes

Twins and horseshoes are both considered lucky. I have twins and I grew up in the country, so for me both symbols have personal meaning. I've brought these symbols together to demonstrate what can happen when two people combine skills, talents, ideas, and passions.

Twin Horseshoes represents the synergy that is created by two people working towards a common goal. It is the creation of something that could never be imagined by either person on their own. It's a form of luck that is made when you are open to new opportunities. It's the sound of 'clinking horseshoes' when things are moving fast, and you just have to hold on tight. It's the joining of forces to create, collaborate, and inspire; the combined magic of two people sharing their energy.

Until recently, becoming published was the most difficult part of writing a book. Now, with the expansion of technology and self-publishing platforms, publishing is available to everyone. But it's not easy and not everyone has the ability, knowledge, or confidence to take this journey on their own. Sometimes we need a cheerleader, a planner, an organizer, and a skilled consultant to guide and motivate us along the way.

That's where I come in. As a published author of numerous articles, blog posts, and bestselling books, I know what it is like to be compelled to write a story simply because it must be told. I use my 15 years of publishing experience to help you through the writing and publishing process from start to finish, so that you get a book you are proud of and have the greatest opportunity for success.

Every story starts with a blank page…let me help you write your story!

I believe that by publishing authentic, diverse stories we can make the world a kinder place to live. Twin Horseshoes is a way for you to publish your unique story with a little help along the way!

twinhorseshoes@gmail.com

www.twinhorseshoes.ca

https://www.linkedin.com/company/Twin-Horseshoes

About the Author
Marcia Allyn Luke

Marcia Allyn has an Honours Bachelor in English from the University of Guelph and a postgraduate Publishing Certificate from Ryerson University. She is currently completing a Master of Professional Education at Western University. Her favourite pastime is reading, and she can often be found with her nose in a book. Marcia has been a writer at heart from the very beginning, writing children's books for younger grades at elementary school. Marcia has contributed to a #1 Bestselling book, *Silent Grief, Healing, & Hope*, and has authored numerous articles for TWINS Magazine, New Dreamhomes Magazine, and Life in Multiples.

Marcia has a passion for education and lifelong learning, devoting her career to publishing educational resources, developing curriculum, and teaching at the post-secondary level. She has been teaching since 2017 and has taught courses such as Introductory Communications, Professional Writing, College English, and Conspiracy Theories (Critical Thinking), at Fleming College, George Brown College, and Humber College. She has 15 years' experience in post-secondary education in a variety of teaching, editorial, marketing, management, and sales positions, providing her with a unique, holistic perspective. Companies Marcia has worked with include American Technical Publishers, McGraw-Hill Education, NELSON Education, and Harlequin Enterprises. Marcia is recognized as digitally savvy and forward thinking and has been invited regularly to pilot and launch new technology, as well as provide training and documentation cross-functionally. She drives change for innovation and efficiency. She is a collaborative and diplomatic leader and team member, and she thrives on a challenge.

Marcia likes to volunteer for causes related to children's and women's rights and donates blood on a regular basis. When not reading, writing, or teaching, Marcia is mom to twin girls. She likes to spend time with family and friends, participate in any activity outdoors, and catch up on sleep whenever possible. Marcia loves coffee, *Harry Potter*, and puppy snuggles.

- "Editor for Life" profile in Boldface, Editors Toronto, 2021.

- Guest Blog Posts on *Brewing Coffee, Twisting Words & Breaking Pencils* in 2021, 2019, and 2016.
- Featured on *The Gifters Podcast* with Christopher Kai, 2020.
- Guest speaker & panelist with George Brown College, Girls Incorporated, Durham College, and Ontario Tech University.

Notes

Here are some other books that have had a profound impact in my life—not an exhaustive list at all, but it's a start. Enjoy!

Atwood, M., & Lee-Merrion, H. (2019). *Oryx and Crake.* London, England: The Folio Society.

Brontë, C., Smith, M., & Atkinson, J. (2019). *Jane Eyre.* Oxford, England: Oxford University Press.

Dostoyevsky, F., Pevear, R., & Volokhonsky, L. (1993). *Crime and Punishment.* New York, NY: Alfred A. Knopf.

Gladwell, M. (2019). *The Tipping Point: How Little Things Can Make a Big Difference.* Boston, MA: Back Bay Books / Little, Brown and Company.

Hinton, S. E. (1988). *The Outsiders: S.E. Hinton* (Reprint ed.). London, England: Speak.

Jonson, B., & Peter, G. J. (2020). *The Alchemist.* Peterborough, ON: Broadview Press.

Levoy, G. (1998). *Callings: Finding and Following an Authentic Life.* London, England: HarperCollins.

Mate, D. G. (2018). *In the Realm of Hungry Ghosts.* London, England: VERMILION.

Plato, Bloom, A. D., & Kirsch, A. (2016). *The Republic of Plato*. New York, NY: Basic Books.

Shen, A. (2016). *Bad Girls Throughout History: 100 Remarkable Women Who Changed the World.* San Francisco, CA: Chronicle Books.

Thomas, A. (2021). *The Hate U Give.* New York, NY: Balzer + Bray.

Truss, L., & Timmons, B. (2007). *Eats, Shoots & Leaves: Why, commas really do make a difference!* New York, NY: Scholastic.

Letters to My Hypothetical Children

www.ingramcontent.com/pod-product-compliance
Lightning Source LLC
Chambersburg PA
CBHW071814080526
44589CB00012B/789